The Grants World Inside Out

The Grants World Inside Out

Robert A. Lucas

UNIVERSITY OF ILLINOIS PRESS
Urbana and Chicago

This book is printed on acid-free paper.

Library of Congress Cataloging-in-Publication Data

Lucas, Robert A.
   The grants world inside out / Robert A. Lucas.
        p.   cm.
     ISBN 0-252-01862-1 (alk. paper)
        1. Universities and colleges—United States—Finance—
Humor. 2. Research grants—United States—Humor. 3. American
wit and humor. I. Title.
PN6231.S3L8   1992
818'.5407—dc20   91-18861
                                                                           CIP

Contents

Preface

The university is supposed to be the wrong place to satisfy a craving for humor. A friend of mine found that out. He worked in the public relations office of a Big Ten university during the student unrest of the sixties. His job was to tape-record a telephone message to keep the public informed whenever something newsworthy happened.

Student demonstrations occurred daily then, and the dial-in was popular. One day, to lighten things up, he folded a humorous quip in with the rest of the news. The vice-president for university relations heard about it and called him in. In a curt interview, he told my friend: "There is nothing funny about the university." He wasn't kidding. Like the warning signs about guns at airline security stations, he wanted it known that any jokes about academe would be treated seriously.

I was impressed with the admonition. For years I joked only in closets. Then one day I wrote a parody of a call for proposals (see "Stalking the Ideal Grant Announcement"), which I shared with some colleagues. A year later I got a call from Gene Stein and Frea Sladek, the new editors of *Grants Magazine*. They had seen the parody and asked if I would edit a column for the journal that chronicled the funny things that happen in the grants office. We settled on the title "Grins in the Grants Office," and I found a crack in the closet door that allowed me to do what the Big Ten vice-president had said ought not be done.

The first column was published in 1981. As time went on, the columns covered the spectrum of activities relating to developing and administering grants in a university environment. A pattern emerged and the columns shaped themselves into a set of readings. It became sensible to think of the collection as a book.

So here it is. I won't be disappointed if some people don't feel comfortable with the jokes. Some of my closest friends still don't accept humor as part of the workplace. This may include my son. Normally a person of sunny disposition, he asked me one day while I was typing away at a column if I was working on an article for "Grims in the Grants Office."

I always knew he was vice-presidential material.

Acknowledgments

I am indebted to many people for their time, energy, and attention to this material as it originated in a series of articles and afterward as it took shape as a book. Thanks must begin with Frea Sladek and Gene Stein, who first suggested that the light side of what happens in research development and administration offices ought to be chronicled in a column in *Grants Magazine.*

I appreciate the editorial freedom they gave me. If I thought a column was funny, that was good enough for them. Such unquestioned support had its downside, of course. I sometimes found myself wondering when I read a column in print what I had thought was funny about it in the first place. It was a little like that strange sense I sometimes have of looking at a Gary Larson cartoon and not getting it. I am therefore grateful to have the opportunity to write this book. It has given me another chance to make sure I got all the jokes.

From the beginning, my good and loyal friend Bob Mc-Donnell read every chapter and helped me shape and sharpen my ideas with his kind questioning. This book will be the more enjoyable because of his unwavering help, support, and encouragement. I also wish to thank Mary Kay Harrington, Bill Rife, John McBride, and Blanchard Hiatt, all of whom gave the final text a careful reading and who made many useful suggestions.

Others who helped in important ways were Margaret Cardoza, Carol Brookshire, Gail Tedford, Marilyn York, Kerry Paulson, Kathy Constantine, John Harrington, Glenn Irvin, Roger Swanson, Bob Dignan, Tom Davis, Al Amaral, Norm Orava, Diana Keeling, Vicki Leon, Danette Davis, Lisa Bosakowski, Jim Squire, Natalie Kirkman, Kathleen Larmett, Paul Zimmer, Don Thackrey, Bob Koob, and Malcolm Wilson.

I want to thank Bob Boice, from whom I learned that if I followed his system of writing I could finish this book before senility overtook me. I leave it to the reader to judge whether I succeeded.

I am grateful to Alan Yang of Cal Poly for permission to print his response to the solicitation of the National Reflection Institute and to Bob Schuerman of Pennsylvania State University, who told me I could share his unique process for avoiding the transmission of viruses through the computing systems as long as I spelled his name right. I also wish to acknowledge the generosity of Plenum Press, publishers of *Grants Magazine*, in which "Grins in the Grants Office" first appeared, for permission to use material from my column as a basis for this book; the Society of Research Administrators for permission to use "Negotiating a True Indirect Cost Rate," which first appeared in its journal; and the National Council of University Research Administrators and Al Sinisgalli for picking up the Ann Granters letters while they were still in manuscript form and printing them in the NCURA newsletter.

This acknowledgment would not be complete without thanking all the people at the University of Illinois Press for their help. At least that's what they told me. I am particularly thankful to Dick Wentworth, who saw the potential in my prospectus for this book, and to Terry Sears, who caught every misplaced modifier and who guided me deftly through the business of completing this book.

Thanks are also due to my family: to my sons, Michael and Daniel, who have tolerated my peculiar behavior wonderfully over the years; to my daughters, Rachel and Rebecca, who are still young enough to think that my behavior is normal; and to my lovely wife, friend, and companion, Wendy, who knows I'm not normal but thinks I'm special anyway.

The Grants World Inside Out

1

Stalking the Ideal Grant Announcement

For years I ran workshops on grant writing in which I said proposals are hard work, and hard work takes time. Sometimes, I said, it takes three years from conception to reception: a year to get an idea and find the right sponsor, a year to write a fundable proposal, and a year to wait for the answer to come.

But most workshop participants wanted quick results. Even though I spent hours explaining how much time and effort it took to get a grant, they hung on to the belief that it had to be easier than all that.

So, always one to please, I concocted a program announcement to satisfy the desire for instant gratification. It read as follows:

THE NATIONAL REFLECTION INSTITUTE

Promising Investigator Program

The National Reflection Institute is offering a series of fellowships (up to $100,000 a year) to researchers who need time to collect their thoughts before writing a proposal for an extended grant. Work is to be done at another location, preferably a low-pressure site where the distractions of academe will not impede rumination.

Funding for the first six months is commensurate with monthly salary, plus relocation costs and a hardship factor for leaving the classroom behind. Laboratory supplies, re-search assistants, and book runners are allowable.

Another six months' support may be granted upon receipt of a postcard indicating that the first six just didn't quite do it. This request will also satisfy the requirement for an interim technical report. Supplemental grants of $25,000 may be requested at any time to fly a colleague to the work site to assist in reflections.

Application consists of a letter with your name, a list of up to ten topics you wish to explore, not limited to your field of expertise, and a single figure for the amount of funds required. Because the NRI does not make grants to institutions, no indirect costs are allowed. Please submit your bank account number with your letter to facilitate direct deposit.

Deadline is continuous. Allow three days for proposal review.

Last year the NRI had funding sufficient for 700 grants. The 300 applications received were approved at the re-quested level. This year the Institute anticipates a 200 per-cent increase in funding.

Whenever I would hand it out, the workshop participants would respond in much the same way. At first they would read casually. Then their eyes would widen. Soon they would be glancing furtively at their neighbors to see if they had picked up on the significance of the announcement.

Then closer inspection, and a pause. The paper would be pushed away, and pulled back. A smile, followed by elbow-poking of the neighbor. "I knew it was a gag all along." And so the joke would be over.

Except for one faculty member. He played along with the scam and wrote a response, which he sent to our office for processing. It went like this:

As noted in your handout, please consider the following as formal application for NRI funding:
Name: Yang, Alan I.

Topics: Cold substance transformation: Lucerne, Switzer-
land
Hedonism as culture: Lake Como, Italy (partially
funded by the Rockefeller Foundation)
Tidal pool ecology: Kaanapali, Maui
Psychological determinants of sushi: Nara, Japan
Social undercurrents prevalent in the samba: Rio
de Janeiro, Brazil

Total requested: $29,850.21

Please note the above list already reflects a 50 percent
reduction in topics from the requested ten. The reflection
which resulted in the above reduction took place at my
residence. Thus, the amount requested is only one-half of
the total due. I feel I am entitled to an immediate payment
of $29,850.21 for reflection already performed.

Thank you for your attention in this matter.

The NRI announcement and Yang's response were printed
in our campus grants newsletter. Shortly after they were published, a faculty member in the School of Engineering called. He
had read the five-part proposal and wanted to know if someone
had really wanted to do that. I told him it wasn't so. He said
he thought maybe it was a gag, but he just wanted to make
sure. Damnedest thing he'd ever read. I assured him that we
would never fund anything like that.

We need humor in the workplace, partly so that more people
can recognize it when they see it, and partly because more humor
would make being a grants administrator easier, especially when
we spend most of our time working with people who are looking
for a grant opportunity that reads like the one for the National
Reflection Institute.

2

Ask Ann Granters

The grants world is a complex and often confusing place. Those who compete in it need real answers to real questions if they are to keep ahead. But most books on grantsmanship skirt the tough questions about how to get and keep grants. Their advice is on a par with what we learned in third grade about how to behave in the lunch line. Not this book. Here Ann Granters answers sensitive questions about how to get and keep grants.

Ms. Granters is as knowledgeable a person as exists in the grants world. Her qualifications include a career as a funded researcher, followed by extensive experience with a federal agency, a major foundation, and two universities. Recently, though, all she does is write a column and consult every so often to keep up payments on her home in Malibu. She must know plenty we don't know.

$ $ $

DEAR ANN: I have heard that some proposals are wired. What does this mean? Is there any advantage to having a proposal wired?

UNCERTAIN

DEAR UNC: Some proposals are wired. You can have yours

wired too. Just take your proposal to your favorite electronics store and ask for a Nobel Wiring Kit. Once your proposal has been hooked up, it will glow with confidence. If you get the souped-up version with voice synthesizer, your proposal will also sing. Proposals that sing get funded. Just don't proofread them in the bathtub.

$ $ $

DEAR ANN: Recently I got a grant for research that had a line item in the budget for a microcomputer. Our procurement office says I have to do a feasibility study to get the purchase approved. Don't you think that's a little ridiculous?

PUZZLED FROM NORMAL STATE U

DEAR NORMAL STATE PUZZLED: What's happening at State is ridiculous. It's also normal. Since you're there, you're going to have to act normal too. Don't push reason. Push paper. That's the way the bureaucrats convince the public that the job you're doing is a professional one.

Why not take a proactive approach? Go back to your purchasing officer, apologize for your erratic behavior, and ask exactly what is required. Then ask if there isn't something else you could do to make your requisition more complete. Call around to the purchasing offices at other universities. Find out some of the extra steps they demand. Then insist on doing these too.

Once you put all this additional information in your order, no one will take the time to actually read what you have written, and you'll be able to use a feasibility study for a Macintosh to justify a CRAY. Everyone will be happy, including the auditor. He may even nominate you for a new and very competitive prize, the Auditor General's John Muir Paper Trail Award.

$ $ $

DEAR ANN: I am an untenured assistant professor and have been told to get a grant. I have never written a proposal before. I went to the full professors in the department, but they were no help. They acted gruff, like if I didn't know how to do it, I should never have been hired in the first place. A friend told me they behaved that way because they themselves never had a grant and had no more idea about how to get one than I do. Do you think this is true?

STYMIED

DEAR STYMIED: Whether it is or not makes no difference. You're the one without tenure, so you're the one with the problem. Fortunately, the solution is relatively simple.

Go to your local stationery store. Ask for a standard grant award form. You'll find it in the section with apartment lease forms, blank certificates of achievement, and model wills. Write in the name of a prestigious foundation and send it to yourself.

Show it to everyone. Then get to work on your grant, but be cagey about telling anyone what you're actually doing. Allude to the need for secrecy because it's an extremely competitive field, and go through the motions of running a project.

When it's about time for you to publish, find an article on your topic in a prestigious journal. Stagger into a departmental meeting with it, distraught and upset. Tell everyone you're devastated because somebody beat you into print with the results.

If the discovery is a big one, you'll get a lot of sympathy, mostly because your colleagues will be relieved that they won't have to put up with the petulant carryings-on of a rising star. Promotion and tenure will follow.

$ $ $

DEAR ANN: I know I shouldn't be writing to you because you have people out there with more serious problems than mine. But I'm a dean, and I want to know what to do with a faculty member who just got a word processor. This guy has been around for a generation without doing a thing. Now he's writing down everything he's thought since 1950.

His latest is a forty-page draft of a foundation proposal for an interdisciplinary general education plan that will integrate knowledge from twenty-three of our thirty-two departments. The proposal argues that we should synthesize the curriculum so that all knowledge is conveyed at once. He's so enamored of the idea that he put a copyright symbol on the front cover and sent it to everyone on the faculty for comment.

People are coming in screaming at me that this thing is so dumb it must be an administrative plot using him as cover.

IN A QUANDARY

DEAR QUAN: What you are witnessing is called random thinking. It has no organized pattern and no particular direction. Random thinking will generate a worthwhile idea now and then. In fact, it comes so close to real thinking, sometimes even the editors at *The National Enquirer* are fooled.

Fortunately, random thinkers are not dangerous. They're just time consuming. Avoid them. A good way to do so is to install a brass gong at the entrance to your office and have a graduate assistant sound it every time they approach. This will both please them and give you time to slip out the back.

If the window is stuck, and you get stuck listening to their ramblings, don't do so for more than five minutes. When you think you've had enough, jerk your head, look at your watch, blurt out "ohmygod," and burst out of the office claiming there's an appointment with the president you forgot.

You'll be safely out the door, and they will spend a few moments pitying your life which is so driven by schedules that you have no time for spontaneity. Then they'll wander off, secretly thankful they didn't have to do anything about the proposal because they just recalled a better idea they had in 1967 and want to get it on hard disk before the muse leaves.

I should alert you, however, to some recent discoveries in random thinking theory. A case study was published about a university where administrators decided that rather than read and consider every proposal for curricular change, they would simply implement every fifth one. They then devoted the energy they would have normally spent on review to explaining to those whose ideas weren't chosen why their ideas were passed over.

The personal touch paid off. Because all faculty members who submitted ideas felt they had had a fair hearing, everyone was agreeable to the changes, and every fifth idea worked out even better than superior ideas had in the past.

Still, I'd be careful with this character. Had the fifth been his idea, your institution might have suffered a serious hangover.

$ $ $

DEAR ANN: I want to write a grant proposal, but I'm hamstrung because my college isn't on BITNET. If we were on it, I could type in a draft of my proposal and get fast feedback from scholars throughout the world. Then I could write a better proposal and get a grant.

STOPPED SHORT

DEAR STOPPED: You're what's known as an "ifweejah." Ifweejahs say things like, "If we just had a certain journal in the library," or "If we just had an insider's list of the basic research priorities of the ten top industries in the state," or "If we just had an institute . . ." For the true ifweejah, the list is endless, but any single item is enough to keep him or her from writing a proposal.

The problem with ifweejahs is that if all the possible obstacles to writing a proposal are removed and they do get a grant, the next thing you hear is, "If we just had an office that handled all the bureaucratic nonsense of running a grant, and if we just . . ."

3

A Grants Glossary: What's the Word?

We've all fumbled for a word now and then, frustrated that we couldn't find the exact one for a thought we wanted to express. Sometimes I've gone to a thesaurus, only to be disappointed that a word I knew must be there wasn't.

As it turns out, not being able to find the right word is not always our fault. Sometimes there is no single word to describe what it is we want to express, even though we feel certain that *le mot juste* must exist.

Scholars now recognize that there are phenomena that truly deserve their own words but have not yet been the beneficiary of the wordsmith's art. A team of lexicographers is even now surveying, gathering, identifying, and (what's the word?) taxonomizing these phenomena and assigning them words.

Some of their results were leaked in the dramatic TV series "Not Necessarily the News." The first official release was published in 1984 under the title *Sniglets (Snig'lit): Any Word That Doesn't Appear in the Dictionary, But Should,* by Rich Hall.

Here are some examples:

> rovalert (ROV ah lert): *n.* The system whereby one dog can quickly establish an entire neighborhood of barking.
> carperpetuation (kar pur PET chu a shun) *n.* The act, when vacuuming, of running over a string or a piece of lint at least a dozen times, reaching over and picking it up,

examining it, then putting it back down to give the vacuum one more chance.

The grants world has some likely sniglet candidates. The following are suggested for consideration:

adminesia (ad mih NEE zee uh): *n.* The mental state assumed by an administrator as he or she claims no recollection of a prior commitment.

argrant (AR grant): *n.* The phenomenon whereby a weird idea orphaned in its proposal stage is adopted by new-found admirers immediately following the announcement of a two-million-dollar grant.

appropriotic (uh PRO pree ah tick): *adj.* Of or pertaining to the penchant to overuse the term "appropriate" in a proposal when the guidelines call for measurable objectives and outcomes and the principal investigator hasn't the foggiest idea what to do. It produces such sentences as: "The project director will take appropriate measures to seek appropriate levels of support for the delivery of appropriate services." Appropriately enough, most such proposals are funded appropriately.

audiotic (aw dee AH tick): *adj.* Of or pertaining to a meaningless procedure followed mainly to please the auditors.

blowprop (BLOH prop): *n.* A proposal written before you have anything to say. It strings together phrases like "tentatively we would hope to explore" in a popcorn chain of empty meaning.

buckschlepp (BUCK schlepp): *v. int.* To trudge around campus with a proposal and buckslip seeking signatures for approval.

chonold (ch'an OLD): *n.* The microblip of sound heard on the phone between the third ring and a sponsor putting you on hold.

colloberation (ko LOB er ay shun): *n.* The phenomenon whereby a number of faculty members refuse to take the lead in writing a major interdisciplinary proposal, browbeat a colleague into doing so, and then later gang up on the writer because he or she hasn't adequately represented their pet areas.

fliar (FLY er): *n.* A brochure that describes a program in much more complimentary terms than it warrants.

gluxit (GLUCK sit): *n.* The act of dropping off the loose ends of a proposal two hours before the express mail pickup, wishing the staff good luck, and then exiting.

grantic (GRAN tic): *adj.* Of or pertaining to the state following "gluxit," usually aggravated by the staff's inability to locate in the guidelines where the sponsor states how many copies of the proposal should be sent.

gradugrunt (GRAD dju gruhnt): *n.* A student hired on a grant to gather research data endlessly.

membler (MEM blur): *n.* A faculty member describing to the vice-president how his or her department will match a grant dollar for dollar.

muddleman (MUH dul man): *n.* The intermediary in a government bureaucracy.

portnastormia (port nah STOR mee uh): *n.* The act of finding yet another trivial task that must be completed before one can start drafting a major proposal.

propout (PROP owt): *n.* The act of grabbing any excuse not to write the same proposal.

propwarp (PROP worp): *n.* The space where a proposal goes after a foundation decides the timing is not right to fund it, but it doesn't want to say no.

simultomania (sy muhl toe MAY nee ah): *n.* The lemminglike drive that periodically compels faculty members to converge on the grants office with simultaneous deadlines.

solipsignorant (sah lip SIG nor ent): *adj.* Of or pertaining to the queasy feeling that you are the only one who didn't know about a major new grant program until a week after the closing date.

stiff (STIF): *n.* A staff of one.

styrofact (STY roh fakt): *n.* A work of art produced by a bored faculty member during a meeting, often etched around the edges of a styrofoam coffee cup.

swaic (SWAYK): *v.* An acronym taken from "Sponsor Won't

Allow Indirect Costs." Usually used in the passive voice, as in, "We sure got swaicked on that foundation grant."

synentropy (sin EN troh pee): *n.* The ability of a proposal-writing committee to produce less as a whole than any of its members could have produced individually in the same amount of time.

swr (SWER): *n.* An acronym taken from "Signed without Reading." Used in the same way as "per" when signing proposals, and signifying about the same thing.

toejam (TOW jam): *n.* An interdisciplinary research project that accretes endless seed grants but produces no results because it always falls between the cracks at the sponsors.

uhmo (UH mo): *n.* Any of a variety of distracted and meaningless grunts made by a campus official in a chance encounter with a faculty member, primarily to indicate that he or she was listening to the proposal idea the person was describing. The professor later references the grunt as approval from the top for a new research thrust and cites it as if it carried the full force of a memorandum.

underhead (UHN der hed): *n.* What's left after overhead.

unnovation (uhn oh VAY shun): *n.* The act of undoing the damage caused by a bad idea implemented on a megagrant.

untimatum (uhn tih MAY tum): *n.* An ultimatum with no teeth in it.

4

Marketing the Modern Proposal

It's a jungle out there, and we've got to keep up on the latest marketing techniques if we're going to sell any bananas. Fortunately that's not too difficult since, in addition to death and taxes, being alive assures us that we will also be the relentless target of somebody else's market strategy.

The lesser mousetrap beats its path to our doors daily, even in the jungle. We need only observe how it gets there to keep abreast of the latest in attention-getting techniques. And if we don't start using some of these techniques ourselves, our competition is going to beat us soundly to the federal agencies.

Concerned that some may already be well ahead of me, at the last conference I attended I skipped the scheduled talks and cruised the halls, chatting with the participants to find out what they were doing about new marketing techniques. I learned a lot.

For instance, one conferee reported that her office improves the package appeal of its proposals by wrapping them in dust jackets, like newly published hardcover books. Then it prints critics' comments on the back of the jacket, like those you would find on any work of fiction, such as: "Burley's best proposal yet"; "A must for any funder's file drawer"; "Sent me scrambling to my spectrophotometer for replication"; "Where has this proposal been all these years?" No one wants to miss out on a best-seller, so the results are a higher yield of grants.

To speed up proposal review, one conferee said her group fresh-dates proposals with words such as "Best when funded by June 1993." Another outfit puts yellow Post-its on the cover sheet with the note, "Give this one top priority — B." Since every sponsor has at least one "B" on its payroll, the proposal gets one more serious look before a final decision is made.

Another university encourages impulse funding by putting a universal product code symbol on the cover sheet of each proposal. All a program officer who is favorably inclined toward a proposal has to do is run the laser wand over the zebra patch and pipe the award down to contracting for a grant.

One grant writer described using a full-court press to play to agency bias. Before sending off a proposal, her office staff prestamps separate copies FILE, PROGRAM OFFICER, SCIENCE BOARD MEMBER, FORMAT CHECKER, SITE TEAM LEADER, TECHNICAL REVIEW TEAM, CONTRACTING OFFICER, and so on. What looks like a courtesy turns out to offer an incredible advantage.

The gambit enables staff to modify copy to fit any known predilections of the recipients. If the program officer is a wine buff, for instance, the staff sprinkles phrases throughout that copy like: "From that little research group nestled in the valley"; "Very fundable"; "Sure to stimulate dinner conversation"; "Don't wait for the arrival of the '93s."

For the jazz buff, the section describing the research team might read: "Billie Coe Efficient on statistics, Eddie Saches on the Cyber, Waters Jordan backing up on socioeconomic impact."

If the proposal passes review, the copy destined for the FISCAL OFFICER reveals the true merit of the system. It has a budget with all figures 20 percent higher than those contained in the rest of the copies.

Another grants officer has figured a way to market proposals incredibly cheaply. Her office has gotten good results for less than ten dollars using classified ads in the *Washington Post*. With some judicious pruning, fifty-page proposals can be cut down for easy reading and funding as follows:

• ATTRACTIVELY PRICED PALEO-MAGNETIC STUDY. RE-

SEARCHER ANXIOUS. ASKING LOW BLUE BOOK. FIRST
$100,000 TAKES.
- NEW MATH DEMO. MINT CONDITION. SECOND OWNER.
SMART! $17,000/OBO.
- 1968 UNIFIED FIELD THEORY: NOT IN RUNNING CON-
DITION. USABLE PARTS. GOOD SECOND LAW, FAIR REL-
ATIVITY. SERIOUS INQUIRIES ONLY.

Another group used the word processor to advantage. It
reported some success taking a turned-down proposal from the
National Science Foundation, issuing a global substitute command on the computer to change the word "ecology" to "pa-
thology," and resubmitting the grant to the National Institutes
of Health.

In the same vein, an engineering professor programmed her
word processor so that all she had to do was identify two or
three buzzwords from the call for proposal. Then she wrote a
macro to highlight each automatically as it appeared. The first
occurrence would be normal, but the second would show up in
boldface; the third, underlined; and the fourth, **boldface underlined.**

Another office has begun mounting a science fair for unfunded proposals. It's an annual rummage sale that combines
the best of the flea market and the swap meet. Those who fund
basic research can't wait for their hand-addressed invitations.
Researchers set up booths in a gymnasium where the bargain
bust features proposals with small irregularities that would cost
tens of thousands more if perfect.

The fair is held in the middle of September to take advantage
of end-of-the-federal-fiscal-year giving. It has been so well received that sponsors are now hanging on to funds just for this
event. Most popular have been the blue-light specials.

An innovative Eastern group tried a completely different
tack. It took scripts from fortune cookies and distributed them
throughout its proposals like "blow-ins," those loose subscription
postcards that fall like dandruff from our magazines. Despite
how hokey the fortunes were, the reviewers couldn't help but
be moved by the messages. Among the most effective were:

"Follow your heart"; "Share what you have with someone less fortunate"; "You will soon take a risk that will make you famous."

A southwestern group (before oil prices took a tumble) had even greater success when it blew in hundred-dollar bills instead of fortune-cookie fortunes.

It's all part of what's happening—the crush of the future that can't be ignored. Ideas that can put your backlog on the front burner. At your local newsstand. For pennies a day. The cost of a stick of low-tar gum. *Be there.*

5

Big Ad Visits the Small Campus

Ever since I heard about a development office that asked potential donors to take out life insurance policies on themselves and name the nonprofit institution as the beneficiary, I knew I would always straggle behind if I didn't get professional help. So one day I dialed the 800-number of a development consultant, Adrian Associates, to see what a professional agency could offer.

The phone was picked up immediately.

VOICE: Hello, this is Adrian, CPF. How may I help you?

ME: Yeah, I'm calling about new approaches in grants, but I'm not very familiar with how development consultants work. Like I don't even know what CPF stands for. What's that mean? Certified Public Fund-raiser, or something like that?

ADRIAN: Nope. Means "Close Personal Friend." We're all CPFs in this business. Keeps us from CPR, if you get what I mean. Haw haw.

ME: Maybe I do. What does it take to become a CPF?

ADRIAN: Just a phone call. Like this. So why don't you call me "Big Ad." All my close personal friends do.

ME: Thanks. I didn't know it could be that simple.

BIG AD: You ain't seen nothing yet, as they say. What brings you to call?

ME: I want to improve the marketing of our research.

BIG AD: Hey, you came to the right place. We do market research every day.

ME: No, I'm afraid you've misunderstood. *We* do research. What we want to do is to market it better.

BIG AD: Okay, so what do you do now?

ME: We write sixty-page proposals and someone sends us money.

BIG AD: So?

ME: So it doesn't happen often enough. The shelf life of our proposals is too long. We need quicker turnover, more grants.

BIG AD: Then don't waste their time. You gotta shorten your pitch. Today's public servants want push-button convenience, armchair shopping, when they want it, where they want it.

    Forget about big proposals. Start with cards and letters, for Pete's sake. If you have to write a long letter, make them think it's short by putting something like "READING TIME: TWO MINUTES" at the top.

    Don't worry about how much time it actually takes to read. When we make our time estimates, we assume everyone has graduated from Evelyn Wood's course, even though we know there are a lot of people out there with eighth-grade reading levels. Most people still move their lips.

ME: Fifth-grade level may be more like it, judging from the reviews I got back on our last set of proposals. They missed half of what was there.

BIG AD: Whatever. Just remember the pitch has got to be quick. You could start with the envelope. Maybe print things on the outside like, "DATED OFFER—ACT NOW," or "THIS PROPOSAL COULD MAKE YOUR CAREER," or "HOW WOULD YOU LIKE TO HAVE GOOD, SOLID RESEARCH FOR JUST HUNDREDS OF DOLLARS A DAY?"

ME: Go on.

BIG AD: Then, inside your envelope, you could put a simple return postcard that says, "NO SALES PITCH. JUST OUTSTANDING RESEARCH, MONTH AFTER MONTH, DELIVERED TO YOUR FILE DRAWER."

    Use those punch-out tokens that they can slip into a slot that says, "FUNDED." Gives them something to do and the illusion of decisive action at the same time.

ME: Sounds good to me.

BIG AD: And don't forget to include one of those sealed letters that says on the outside, "OPEN THIS ONLY IF YOU DECIDE TO DECLINE THIS IRRESISTIBLE OFFER."

ME: Good idea. I don't know how many of those buggers I've fished out of the wastebasket just to make sure I hadn't missed something.

BIG AD: Now you're catching on. Make them feel special. When you send out a prospectus, you gotta let them know it's more than just a proposal. Make them think if they fund you, they'll be going with an organization that's so far out on the frontier of knowledge that it's publishing reports on data that hasn't even been collected yet.

ME: Tell me more.

BIG AD: Everyone wants to be a winner, for nothing if possible. Where would *Reader's Digest* be today if all they ever sent you were subscription blanks?

ME: You mean those sweepstakes are really magazine drives?

BIG AD: See what I mean about eighth-grade reading level?

Look, you can do the same kind of thing. Tell 'em your computer goofed and generated fifty regression analyses that you don't know what to do with, and they're going at incredibly low prices. Or put a teaser on your envelope that begins:

You may have already won at least . . .
- 400-page report
- doctoral thesis
- matching grant

ME: You know, this does sound like it has possibilities. How long would it take for you to put together an approach for us?

BIG AD: It won't be easy. Can I have till Monday?

It was Friday. I said okay, and figured he worked weekends.

Three days later Big Ad dropped off a sixteen-page typeset plan, bound in a folder, no more than a hundred words per page, wide margins, and lots of bullets.

He left as quickly as he arrived.

He was smaller than I had pictured him.

As I opened the package I trembled that what I would find

would be page after page of ad glib: "All this and more . . . And that's not all . . . Here's why . . . So let's look at the record . . . We're sure you'll agree there's an even better way . . . Sound incredible? Sound fantastic? Well, this is only the beginning . . . We've saved the best for last . . . It's just part of the story . . . The opportunity of a lifetime with a three-step formula that guarantees success no matter how little you have . . . No questions asked."

My fears were unfounded.

What unfolded startled me with its simplicity. Big Ad proposed a complete grant-marketing system built around membership, product identity, and solid follow-through.

"Join our Proposal-of-the-Month Club," the package read.

> For only $29,995, you can choose three complete research projects from the ten exciting possibilities pictured here.
>
> As a member of the club, you'll receive a brochure each month describing the featured selection and alternate. If you want to support the research, you simply do nothing. You will be sent the protocol and a complete budget (with a modest indirect cost service charge) at fantastic club savings. You will be charged in convenient monthly installments.
>
> Your only obligation is to fund three research projects within the next twelve months. As a valued member, you will receive regular special offers and the benefits of a bonus plan.

The package went on to describe the scheme. There were no cheap monogrammed sunvisors, coffee mugs, or paperweights. For this guy, videotape players would have been stocking stuffers. Big Ad proposed a coupon worth $10,000 in research bonuses. It could be used to upgrade a master's thesis to a doctoral dissertation, or for a free secondary analysis of current data. For only $20,000 in coupons you could volunteer to be a human subject in a combined archaeological dig/stress reduction experiment in Tahiti.

Central to keeping club members happy was never letting them wonder whether they had made the right decision. As soon as they accepted a grant, they were congratulated for their positive action (the same way manufacturers tell you as soon as you open the box how smart you were to select their food processor): "Congratulations on having chosen Solid State U for your research needs. You have joined the ranks of a select group of prestigious sponsors. If you treat your new principal investigator with care, you will be rewarded with month after month of excellent research and regular reports."

For big grants, Big Ad proposed a special option: sending a PR group to interview sponsors as if they were the coach of a team that had just won the Sugar Bowl. With microphone in hand and the White House in the background, the proposed patter would be as follows: "Tell me, Mr. Public Trust, just what was going through your mind the moment you decided to make that $5.4 million, three-year award? What were your feelings?"

I bought the whole package and sent it immediately to our best sponsors.

The first response came back with blazing speed. It had a teaser on the envelope—a picture of a little television set. The screen said: "And now, a word from your sponsor."

The TV screen was perforated around the edges. If I pried it loose, I could lift it up and peer underneath. I did. Through a glassine window I looked into the letter and read:

"Don't take us for granted."

6

Ask Ann Granters Some More

DEAR ANN: This letter is in response to the guy who said he'd get a grant if they were just on BITNET. That's not my problem. I want a grant in the worst way, but my department chair keeps holding me back.

There's this competition coming up to establish a center to provide extended education to outlying school districts. I'm in electronic engineering, and I figure if we can get the contract, I can set up a remote satellite operation that will give my EE majors a lot of good experience installing and operating electronic equipment. But the Powers That Be won't turn me loose. They think the people in the education department might not follow through.

COLLARED

DEAR COLLARED: Funny you should sign yourself that way, because that's the way your administrators may be thinking about the whole business. Center grants are like dogs. You need to check the size of the paws on those puppies before you bring one home. While they're young and someone else is paying for the shots, they're a lot of fun. But when they grow up, they can be twice as big as you ever imagined and eat you out of department and laboratory.

The problem is that once you get a center, you can't get rid of it without a great deal of personal anguish. Since every center year is equal to about three human ones, you better look closely before you take another step.

There's a good rule for testing how badly you want a center grant. Just ask yourself if when you got it you would be willing to give its associate director your reserved spot in the parking lot.

$ $ $

DEAR ANN: Every time I write a proposal and take it to the grants office, it sits there for weeks. Then the people call me up with a lot of questions about space and cost sharing and other dumb stuff I don't understand. Are these serious problems or are they just hassling me?

WONDERING

DEAR WON: It doesn't make any difference whether or not these are real problems. You yourself have a serious problem that you don't seem to recognize.

Nobody but nobody takes a proposal into the grants office weeks in advance. That's asking for trouble. Here's what you do.

About a month before the deadline, stop by the grants office. Tell them a proposal is coming, but don't say when. Tell them people in different departments are drafting material and you're collaborating with a university down the pike. Hint that you'll drop off a draft as soon as you get something that's in good enough shape for them to look at. But for Pete's sake, don't do it.

Why? Well, think about the way restaurants treat you. They know that the sooner they bring you your lunch, the more time you'll have to find things wrong with it. So they stall, knowing that the more ravenously hungry you are when your food arrives, the less likely you are to send it back to the kitchen. Even if your patty melt tastes like Pogo, when it finally comes, you'll be so grateful you'll just unhinge your jaws and swallow.

If you want to get your proposal off campus expeditiously, treat the grants office people the same way the restaurants treat you. Bring them breadsticks and crackers. Refill their water glasses endlessly. But don't produce the proposal until the very last minute. Then they will have to find a really egregious error to make you change anything. Most probably they'll sign it in desperation, and you'll be out the door in no time at all.

The best part is you can tell everyone you were in close touch with the grants office, and if anything goes wrong, you can blame it on those clowns who never read anything they sign.

$ $ $

DEAR ANN: I'm having a problem getting a grant. I have had seven proposals turned down. The program officers for the sponsors keep coming up with lame excuses for not funding them, like I should try to identify my objectives and list them all in one place, or tie my budget in with my methodology, or some other nonsense.

Ann, my ideas are just too all-encompassing to fit the pigeonholes these niggling bureaucrats come up with. I think I'm being denied a grant because my ideas are radical and challenge the established order. A friend of mine who lectures regularly at a community college in the West thinks my ideas are the best thing since Velikovsky. Should I go to my congresswoman and tell her I'm being given the runaround?

UNNOTICED

DEAR UNNOT: Often program officers, although they are highly competent technically, are not mature enough emotionally to handle the situation you describe. They keep trying to explain what they mean by using arcane concepts such as "detailed methodology," "review of the literature," and stuff like that.

Don't be too hard on them. It's not often they run into someone like you. They deal in cliché. You are an original. Indeed, in the larger order of things it may be important to the balance of the universe that you not be funded. Then your ideas can't be tarnished by association with the established order.

Go West, young man. Join your friend at that community college. You can read Velikovsky to each other.

$ $ $

DEAR ANN: A small local firm has asked me to consult on some management issues. I know zip about consulting. Do you think I should do it? Isn't giving out advice risky?

ON THE VERGE

DEAR ON: Not at all. Being a consultant is a great life. It's like being a grandparent. You get to play with a company's brainchild, dandle it on your knee, and chuck it under the chin. Then when it fills its pants, you can hand it back to management.

Go for it. And remember, the more you charge for a day's consultation, the less likely it is that management will treat you like an employee.

7

Innovations in the Modern Grants Office

The brochure describing the services that our grants development office offers claims that when it comes to advances in grants administration, innovation is just another word for coming in on Monday morning. We didn't get that motto from a public relations firm. We got it by attending to complaints that our practices and procedures were arcane and needed to be updated.

We began with a bold plan to give faculty members already versed in the mechanics of grantsmanship quicker administrative service. We installed a drive-up window. Now researchers can have their proposals checked for budget accuracy and protection of vertebrate animals without having to leave their Volvos. Daily you can hear voices on the intercom saying things like, "Gimme a no-cost time extension on the laser project and hold the audit."

Our insurance agent discouraged us from adding car-side service on roller skates, so we followed the drive-up window with another logical extension—a grants autoteller. The walk-up system is built right into the wall next to the drive-up. Those whose schedules demand maximum flexibility can get quick cash whenever they need it for the all-night supplies store. Like the hot-air hand dryer in the public restroom, the sign reads, "This handy grant dispenser is placed here as a convenience. Fresh money is always available at the touch of a hand. And it leaves no unsightly paper trail that can cause dis-ease. 60 Hz, 120 V, 20 Amps."

Procurement was a bottleneck. Bidding requirements and feasibility studies so overlapped each other that the paperwork was only microns away from sucking its initiators into an infinite loop. Faculty members were bound by red tape that would have made Prometheus look like a rolling stone.

With one stroke of administrative genius, we cut through the Gordian knot of bureaucratic gridlock. We opened an express checkout lane. Now faculty who need six or fewer Macintoshes can have them in their shopping carts and out the door in a matter of minutes. For our shoppers' convenience, we are adding lottery ticket sales, all proceeds to benefit education.

Another innovation came from watching the orderlies on "St. Elsewhere" steer critically ill patients deftly down the hospital halls. Their practiced procedures suggested we could improve our emergency response plan for proposal processing. We role-played scenarios and worked out a series of short-deadline drills.

Now when faculty members stagger in at the last minute with the bits of a travel application to the German Vagesbund Fund, triage is ready when they are. Margaret scans the idea for vital signs, I take the paper's pulps, Kathy slips in a fresh floppy, Kerry fires up the ten-key, and Danette retrieves the final guidelines. If the idea looks like it has a chance of survival, we can refine the narrative, develop a budget, and duplicate final copy all in less than thirty-eight minutes, communicating solely via eyebrow signals above our face masks.

Although the drill has improved our performance considerably, many proposals survive the deadline only to succumb to pneumonia in the peer review process.

Other innovations have taken less work to implement. For those on a diet, we programmed our graphics software packages to generate only low-cal pie charts. For the faculty members who sell short when they quote our indirect cost rate, we have introduced the bonded contract administration option. Based on the premise that anyone who thinks 10 percent is enough overhead to administer a grant must know a whole lot more about our business than we do, we offer hassle-free lack of service.

Under this innovative plan, the grantees are given complete freedom to administer the project within the dollars allotted. In return they post bond in the amount of the grant and sign a statement that frees the university from liability for any disallowance, malpractice, or fraud. In one swoop, these faculty members get what they want, which is our office out of their way, and six months later we get what we want, which is a penitent person who guarantees that he or she will never again quote low rates for indirect costs if only we will take the mess they've created off their hands.

For the fitness-minded, we offer a short course on proposal writing from the back of a cutaway two-ton sound truck. As the flatbed chugs around campus, busy grant recipients can jog behind it and keep up while keeping fit as they master the skills of grants development in a dozen twenty-five-minute circuits.

The gambit also saved us money. We found we could cancel our contract with the man in the white uniform who used to cruise campus ringing bells and distributing the latest grant guidelines. Now fresh guidelines are delivered daily, newspaper style, from the flatbed.

The bells were driving people crazy anyhow.

8

Innovations Better Left Untried

Useful changes in the grants office aren't easy to come by. For every one that works, five don't pan out. Our office has implemented its fair share of clunkers. And just as any good researcher publishes negative results to warn others away from wasting their time, so it seems a good idea to chronicle some of the innovations that didn't fly for us and would be better left untried.

- Instituting a payroll deduction plan for researchers to pay back grant overruns.
- Writing to ten-year-old guidelines to salvage ten-year-old ideas.
- Printing a declaration on the cost-volume section of a Request for Proposal response that states, as the refrigerator repairman does at the front door, "WARNING: Opening this proposal constitutes agreement to award a minimum of $39,995, parts and labor extra."
- The one-minute grants manager.
- Printing a proposal on chemically impregnated paper that begins to smell rank after it's been left in a sponsor's file drawer for more than two months without action.
- Putting proposals into transmittal envelopes to federal sponsors that read: "You may have already made a grant! Open this envelope to learn about a dynamic idea and to read

copies of correspondence between our governor and congressional representatives!"
- Including with your proposal a self-addressed, stamped envelope for the foundation grant check.
- Printing synopses of proposal ideas on postcard-sized blurbs, shrink-wrapping them fifty at a time, and sending them to agency directors. (Shrink-wrapping doesn't work even for the National Institute of Mental Health.)
- Attempting to draw more attention to a proposal by wrapping it with bright yellow two-inch-wide plastic tape that says, "WARNING: This wrapper cannot be removed except by funder," and then breaking the seal.
- Abstaining from sex for five days before writing a proposal.
- Putting "Lemon Fresh" on the front cover of a proposal as a passive-aggressive protest against a principal investigator you don't like.
- Awarding one month of valet parking to the most successful grantsperson of the year. (Your grants development office won't be able to keep up with the increased proposal activity.)
- Repackaging the parts of proposals that didn't get funded into a half-price package called "Best 'o Grants."
- Hustling interest by sending a flyer to agencies advertising a special: "All research $10,000 below administrator's invoice."
- Remaindering proposals through the U.S. Government Printing Office bookstore.
- Trying to make proposal development more efficient by taking preliminary budget data from a faculty member over the phone, typing it directly into a spreadsheet software program, and then switching control over to a computer that calculates the budget and says through voice mail, "The ball park figure is . . ."
- Recording summaries of proposals on 45-rpm disks that say "Fund me, fund me" when played backward.
- The one-minute grants manager.
- Administering a psychological assessment instrument before opening a project account for a new principal investigator to test his or her sense of fiscal responsibility. (If you can't

resist trying this idea, I suggest you avoid questions like: "As a child, did you often ask for an advance on your allowance? How many years in the hole did you get? Do you believe academic freedom and laissez-faire economics are the same? Have you ever admired a white-collar criminal?")

- Sending "subscription" notes sewn into the binding of monthly technical reports offering reduced rates for continuation if the sponsor renews the research grant now.
- Wholesaling.
- Raising money for seed grants through the campus underground by selling copies of the vacation schedules of the department chair, the dean, and the vice-president for business.
- Putting multiple cover sheets on proposals for film grants that list, in order: project director, proposal producer, co-principal investiga-tors, grant devel-oper, budget devel-oper, budget check-er, typist, special graphic effects, reg-ular graphic effects, graphic effects, graphics, effects, duplicator, pack-ager, hand carrier, filer, mailer, grip, grunt, paper by Hammermill, staples by Swingline.

> Sidebars of excerpts don't work.

- Mimicking "truth in packaging" by identifying who really wrote the proposal, stating something like "as told to Ed Marcella" on the title page.
- Sending a letter to collaborators that threatens two years of turndowns if the recipient doesn't subcontract one grant and send a copy of the letter to six others within a week.
- Offering three-day weekends in Bethesda, Maryland, as proposal-writing incentives.
- Playing tapes of Scrooge's dream sequence in *A Christmas Carol* as telephone background fill-in when you put a sponsor on hold.
- Highlighting pithy excerpts of your proposals by printing them as sidebars.
- Emphasizing the international sensitivity of your research by inserting an interlinear translation in your proposal.
- Putting "$3.00" in the upper right corner of the cover sheet,

as mail order catalogs do, to suggest that the proposal, even if turned down, still has par value.

- Arguing with the National Endowment for the Arts that making a grant without including indirect costs is like commissioning a painting and only paying for the oil and canvas.
- Dramatizing the argument that indirect costs are real costs by billing faculty members for editing, typing, duplicating, and mailing after their proposal has been turned down.
- The one-minute grants manager.
- Toadying to the bias of an agency by writing things like "Composed entirely of recycled ideas" on the cover sheet of a proposal to the Environmental Protection Agency. Even worse is concluding the proposal: "Please dispose of thoughtfully."
- Programming your word processor so that it automatically changes the future tense of the verbs into the past tense, thereby enabling you a year later to turn the proposal into your final report.
- Stuffing an annual giving solicitation letter in with each proposal in case a foundation can't make a grant but still wants to give you a little something.
- Giving campus awardees T-shirts that say, "Ask me about my grant."
- Charging a reshelving fee of 10 percent for each Request for Proposal returned unfunded after you were guaranteed it wasn't wired to the outfit you were sure it was and it was.
- Printing tide charts and the phases of the Moon on the blank pages of your proposal.
- Printing pictures of missing faculty members who never got a grant in the same places.
- Printing clipout coupons on those same pages for offers on college sweatshirts and mugs.
- Printing double coupons in the same places.
- Computing a real-time indirect cost rate. One campus negotiated a computer program with the Department of Health and Human Services that would crank out a new overhead rate daily, incorporating up-to-date costs from the integrated financial management data base. A dedicated campus phone

number announced the rate the same way the telephone company tells us what time it is when we dial POPCORN. The system won the Spruce Goose Prize of the International Nonovation Society for the bureaucratic procedure most vividly embodying the triumph of design over function.

- The one-minute grants manager.
- Asking for a doggie bag when your grant ends with a surplus.
- Putting "From Concentrate" on the cover of proposals that exceed sponsor page limit.
- Giving the address of a mail order research house to sponsors who think your proposal budget is too high.
- Trying to justify a big budget by arguing that costs are slightly higher west of the Rockies, west of the Mississippi, west of the Potomac, or west of anywhere. Even the National Geographic Society doesn't care.
- Carrying computer hacker insurance. (If anything happens, you're just out of luck. Good hackers are hard to replace.)

$ $ $

With all these caveats, so many demands, and only so much time, how can we possibly improve things in the grants office? Simple: The one-minute grants manager.

9

The Right Paper for the Right Proposal

An announcement of a Request for Proposal recently arrived in my office stating that all responses had to be typed on "one-sided pages." I hadn't run into that requirement before. It might have been a koan, like "What is the sound of one hand clapping." It set me to thinking, as koans are supposed to—or aren't supposed to—I forget which.

Where would I find one-sided paper? And if I could, would I want it? Working with one-sided pages could be dangerous. I might carelessly flip over a sheet, uncover a black hole, and disappear forever into negative space. Bad news, except that maybe the auditors couldn't find me, unless they're the ones who invented negative space in the first place.

My dilemma was solved when our insurance carrier said no way did our risk management program cover one-sided pages.

So I was safe, except that the odd phrase set me to thinking about the very material on which we write our proposals. Paper. It's usually white, eight-and-a-half by eleven inches in size, perhaps carrying a watermark. To this starkly simple medium we affix our hopes for millions of dollars.

Maybe we should pay more attention to the paper we use. Bankers do. They print my checks on small slips of paper with pastel panoramas of seashores and mountains, and they don't seem to have to write a proposal every time they want a few dollars.

So it might be a good idea to write proposals on paper that reinforces our message. Following our banker's lead, a proposal to the Department of Commerce could be typed on paper lightly inked with eau de savings bonds. Or a proposal to the Department of Housing and Urban Development could be duplicated on paper with a simulated blond oak panel finish.

I visualize attracting the rapt attention of a Forest Service peer review panel by scribbling the abstract for an arson prevention program on the inside of a matchbook cover. Meanwhile, across the street at the international desk of the Department of Agriculture, a program officer would be ruminating about whether a proposal for research on sheep needs a second review by the animal welfare committee because it is written on vellum.

How about the mathematical and physical sciences directorate of the National Science Foundation? Would they welcome a proposal printed on a Möbius strip, or would they find it a transparent ploy to circumvent the fifteen-page limit?

The Department of Defense, they say, regularly funds proposals that aren't printed on paper at all but consist entirely of multicolored overlays bound between tabbed dividers, three overlays to a division, six divisions to a proposal, thank you, and bring an extra projector bulb, please.

People in the Grants Belt (that area 50 miles either side of a line drawn 300 miles southwest from a point just outside downtown Boston) report that the National Endowment for the Arts likes proposals jotted on placemats from trendy coffee houses. Said one successful grant-getter: "Used to be when we got a grant, the Endowment would cut our budget so bad it was like the guy who says 'Let's have lunch' and then only picks up the tip. Now they're popping for the whole meal. They finally got the message that we are not only hungry but upscale to boot." Their success has some researchers using cocktail napkins to write to the National Institute on Drug Abuse and Alcoholism.

Any proposal could be enhanced with watermarks. I can see a definite edge for one printed on bond with a watermark that says subliminally, "FUND ME."

Size and shape of paper may be relevant as well. One nonprofit agency tried printing all its proposals on paper slightly larger than the eight-and-a-half by eleven. The staff figured that the proposal, like a cardsharp's aces, would stick out from the stack and get better treatment. But they learned that neatniks tended to shuffle bigger proposals to the bottom of the stack, so they reversed the procedure, shaved a sixteenth of an inch off each edge, and found their success rate increased by 23 percent.

Even pop-up pages can be useful. A group of peace advocates finally got a proposal funded when it added a center page that opened up juvenile book–style into a mushroom cloud.

On our campus we've had some success getting basic research grants from industry by appealing to their desire for results. These proposals have only one line per page—the bottom line. This simpler approach reinforces the notion that our ideas have industrial strength.

To dress up solid but undistinguished ideas, we tried to convey the idea of spontaneity of genius by typing them on the backs of envelopes, but the proposals were too hard to bind. So we made their very humdrummedness a strength. We cut the budget, added an unknown principal investigator, and typed each page on sheets that had heavy black bars across the top and bottom of each page, like the cans of nonbrand foodstuffs at the outlet grocery.

We call it the generic proposal format. Every page clobbers the reader with the message that no-name researchers and no-frills proposals mean rock-bottom prices, suitable for the every-day needs of the sponsor. And it works. With it, the grants come in faster than normal—even though the indirect cost rate we use on these is 10 percent higher than our normal rate.

One final note on paper and packaging. The Kellogg Foundation recently stated that enclosing boxtops with proposals no longer gives one a competitive edge. Said a weary foundation executive: "We simply assume that no one planning to write a proposal would consider starting the day without a bowl of cereal, milk, and fruit."

10

Ann Granters at Home

DEAR ANN: I took a proposal in the other day for review, and the grants office said it would take five days to move it through the system and get all the signatures. What's the deal? I didn't have a fixed deadline, but I thought the office ought to move faster than that.

SPEEDY

DEAR SPEED: No problem. You can move a proposal through as fast as you want. Just ask if your grants office offers express proposal approval service. You can usually get twenty-four hour turnaround for about fifty bucks for the first ounce and fifteen for each additional ounce.

$ $ $

DEAR ANN: I know this is a little out of your line, but recently I got information back from the faculty interest file in the grants office that suggests someone in the biology department is the person I've been looking for all my life, not for an inter-disciplinary research partner, but for the other kind. The problem is that I'm so out of it socially that I'm afraid to pursue this lead. What do you suggest?

PARALYZED

DEAR PARA: Have you ever heard of free writing? It's a technique that those who have writing blocks use to get the flow going. They write nonstop for fifteen or twenty minutes, putting down whatever comes into their mind without looking back, rewriting, or revising.

The material is not organized, not ordered in any way. There is not even the expectation that the output will be used in an article. The person just writes to stimulate the creative juices, which have often been stopped up by lack of use or fear of failure. The practice seems to work well for eliminating writing blocks in many people.

I suggest a modification of this process for you. Before you call the biologist, stop on your way home from campus at a ferny bar. Make sure it's a noisy one, with a basketball game showing on the projection TV and a tray full of those tiny weenies you spear with a toothpick and dip into ketchupy sauce.

Go up to the first person you meet and start talking. Say whatever comes into your head, without thinking, without wondering about whether it makes any sense. Don't strive for coherence. Just keep talking. Loud. If you find that you have nothing to say, just keep repeating "I have nothing to say" until something besides that comes out. Do this for fifteen minutes. Then leave.

Once you are home, call up that biologist. Then start. Don't worry about sounding coherent. You will.

$ $ $

DEAR ANN: Everyone seems to be getting ahead except me. I never get my proposals written, and the department thinks I have all sorts of time to do the things the rest of my colleagues don't want to do. I'm on seven committees, but none of them is important. My career is in jeopardy. What do you recommend?

FRAZZLED

DEAR FRAZ: You're probably too available. You need to make an immediate change in your work patterns. From now on, don't go to your campus on alternate Mondays-Tuesdays-Wednesdays and Wednesdays-Thursdays-Fridays. On those days, make sure you place calls to your laboratory assistant, your department chair, your dean, and the people at the agencies where you want to get grants.

Call from the phone booth at your local airport. Hold the phone away from your mouth so people will have to ask you to speak louder. Then shout over the sound of flight announcements and courtesy telephone pages. Abruptly cut off every third conversation, saying you're sorry but you have to run because your flight's just been called.

Do this for about three months. If you get sick of driving to the airport, make a recording of the terminal sounds and play the tape in the background while you call from home.

Your department will soon reevaluate your status. Shortly, you should get released time for pursuing the research you've been describing only in snatches on the phone, and you'll be on your way to an illustrious career of grants, contracts, and preferment.

$ $ $

DEAR ANN: In a critique of a proposal turndown, one reviewer said this about my ideas for institutionalizing the grant: "The writer's plans for continuing the grant after termination of external funds are as visionary as the proposal itself." I'm not sure whether this was a compliment or a complaint. Does it mean I should keep my plans the same way or revise them when I resubmit?

PUZZLED

DEAR PUZZLED: The statement can mean one of two things: either your proposal does what few others do, which is to propose a realistic plan for keeping the activity going once the grant runs out, or else the smoke you've blown in the proposal is equally distributed throughout. I haven't the foggiest, but I've got a hunch.

$ $ $

DEAR ANN: I want to collaborate with another scholar doing secondary analysis of data already gathered, but I'm paralyzed with fear that in switching the floppies back and forth, my machine might contract a computer virus.

NERVOUS

DEAR NERVOUS: I can't blame you. It's important to practice safe computing. Before you insert your floppy disk, make sure you cover it with a sandwich-sized plastic baggie. This will prevent the transmittal of any virus. Then you can go on conceiving great ideas and generating great proposals knowing that you've done your best to act responsibly.

$ $ $

DEAR ANN: I've come into a dry period. I used to get a grant every three tries or so. But my last seven proposals have been turned down flat.

I'm afraid I'm out of touch with the field, over the hill, in the barn, asleep in the hayloft. How do I get back on the highway?

MORIBUND

DEAR MORI: The situation is not as desperate as you think. It may only be that your unconscious is in park. Put it in drive by practicing visualization.

Set aside some time to relax and meditate in a quiet place. Think about grants. Picture them as millions of krill. Then imagine yourself as a blue whale. See yourself cruising the coast, effortlessly scooping thousands of these creatures into your maw.

Then imagine rain. See it turning solid. Imagine some of those solid pieces as round, thick, and gold. Imagine yourself effortlessly gathering these pieces into baskets.

Then picture yourself in a research laboratory—huge like a steel mill. Visualize people lined up at the entrance at 6:45 in the morning, lunch boxes under their arms, thermoses full of coffee, waiting to punch clocks and crank out results.

Do these exercises daily for four weeks. If things don't turn around, try sensory deprivation. Put yourself in an underground cave for three to six months. Then try the steps listed again. They may not work, but the notoriety you will have achieved by trying these unorthodox procedures may bring you funding anyway.

11

The Right Word for the Right Proposal: A Jargon Generator

Nothing produces writer's block more quickly than realizing you're not clear about what you want to say. One cure is to focus on jargon in the early stages and to worry about meaning later. You can do it easily with a jargon generator.

Philip Broughton of the Public Health Service allegedly invented this approach, of which what follows is a new and improved version. Its use is simplicity itself. When you're stuck for something to say in a proposal, you just check the chart and draw a random word from columns A, B, and C. Put the three words together in order and you'll have a string of vocables that will substitute for thought in almost any situation.

The system produces such useful phrases as "optimized logistical factors" and "paradigmatic developmental matrix" with ease. The phrases may not mean anything, but they sound great in proposals. In fact, the system works so well (that is, it produces *viable organizational concepts* so easily) that you may discover ideas you never thought of using. It's like going shopping.

Column A	Column B	Column C
integrated	programmable	network
proactive	organizational	flexibility
time-phased	incremental	analysis
reconfigured	facilitative	model
paradigmatic	real-time	system

Column A	Column B	Column C
parallel	logistical	factor
ongoing	strategic	intervention
functional	responsive	concept
synchronized	hands-on	capability
codified	parametric	matrix
balanced	operational	contingency
optimized	interdisciplinary	interface
viable	digitized	prototype
automated	third-generation	analogue
indexed	holistic	module
cost-effective	developmental	projection
goal-oriented	open-ended	management
down-sized	synergistic	modology
user-friendly	state-of-the-art	paradigm

12

The Role of the Paranormal

Most grants offices publish a bulletin that lists funding opportunities and upcoming deadlines. But faculty members don't win Nobel Prizes just because one grants office does a better job of skimming the *Federal Register* than the next. They win because their grants office has kept them aware of the extrasensory factors that can affect the outcome of their applications.

Even though these factors are invisible, the more advanced grants offices are keeping their researchers tuned in to their influence. Some are printing information about them in their monthly grants bulletins.

A regular column can serve several purposes. It can help faculty members decide if they should follow up on a grant-writing opportunity, change a research direction, or sit down immediately and write a final report. The monthly feature also gives grants offices another way to convey messages of interest and importance to the faculty.

Here are samples from recent grants bulletins:

Beemer—The One Who Has It: June 20–July 19
This is a good month to take out that brie of a turndown that has been ripening in your file and send it out again. Have a contest in your graduate seminar for a new acronym. Now that you are a full professor, it doesn't matter whether your proposal gets funded or not, so your chances for success are

increased 30 percent. You might even suggest that the sponsor use the same reviewers who said ten years ago that your idea was not feasible.

Oudryiam—The Camel: July 20–August 19
    You are entering a dry period for producing useful laboratory results. The drought may last seven years.
    Go to the laboratory. On each of seven days, sacrifice seven rats and seven mice. Before using your microscope, turn around three times and murmur the name of a Nobel Prize winner quietly to yourself. Do not speak to anyone until you read this column again.

Fortunata Septima—Tunnel's Light: December 21–January 20
    Your string of proposal rejections will end this month. Soon grants will proliferate like cobwebs in a barn. You will experience the exquisite stress of writing reports, signing payroll rosters, and filling out purchase requisitions. These duties may seem a nuisance, but do not ignore them.
    Your lucky number continues to be area code 202.

Manyanatus Manyanata—The Dawdler: Tomorrow and Tomorrow and Tomorrow
    Do not reorganize your file system. You did that last summer. Do not revise your freshman lectures. You did that last month.
    This is the month to write that proposal. Do it.
    If you have no idea where to start, try this. Go to the library. Dig up a management text at least forty years old. Find a method for structuring organizations you've never heard of. Summarize it. Add voice mail and a management information system. Draw administrative flow charts on a Macintosh using those shadows that lift the idea right off the page. Say something about the United States entering the postproductivity era. Give the system a catchy title, draft a proposal, and mail it off.
    You'll feel better, we'll feel better, and the concept is sure to come as news to half your peer reviewers.

Allegro—The Flighty One: January 2-5 and 9-10, February 7-9, March 11-15 and 23-27, April 29–May 3, May 16-20, June 8-15,

July 12-23, September 26-29, October 1-3, 5-7, and 18-22, November 6-9, 13-15, and 17-18, December 5-6 and 9-13

Your frequent flier status is in a holding pattern. Conference attendance has fallen off. If you don't get out of your laboratory soon, your flight upgrades will stagnate in coach.

Hunt up a conference. Don't wait for a jumbo fare. Call 805-546-8612 for travel reservations. Ask for Carol. Mention this column.

Acadambo—The Brash One: May 21–July 22

You will be in an unaccountably good mood this month. Don't fight an impulse to take flowers and candy to someone in the grants office. While you're there, tell them you're sorry. Never mind why. Just do it. They'll know.

Parta Animalia—MacThink: Third Tuesday Every Month

The animal welfare committee will be a bear this month. Avoid using any research animal that appears in the first six signs of the zodiac. Try revising your protocol to employ robots instead of animals. Toys 'Я' Us has an electronic monkey that's terrific. It may serve most of your needs for research at half the maintenance cost.

If that doesn't work, take your project to the human subjects committee. Changes in federal regulations have made people a lot easier to use than animals. Caution: Some human subjects are beginning to demand equal treatment. You can let them out for exercise in the afternoon, but don't let them bully you into fresh water and a change of paper every day.

BONUS: Baccalaureatus Atlastus—The Graduate: June 15

Plastics.

Paraparanoid Schitzonoidus—The Untenured One: ∞

You're doing just fine. In fact, you're producing more than anyone around you. Stop feeling guilty because you had that coffee break last month. Relax. Nobody noticed. Take another one this month. Ask someone to join you. Don't worry, he won't talk about how you're slacking off.

Your best time continues to be early morning. Staying up

all night gives you a jump on your best time. Try to forget sleeping altogether. Keep up this pace for five more years.

Ignore double messages you may be receiving concerning expectations and performance.

Bougainvillea—Flower Child: November 21–December 20

One of your graduate students will report the loss of the soles of his sneakers. Check around your laboratory for seepage of toxic chemicals. Is there still tile on the floor? Do the work benches still have legs? Is your laboratory still there?

When you find out where all the soles have gone, you may also discover what has happened to the research data you've been losing.

Tota Thumba—Mittens: January 21–February 20

On the third day of the third week of this month, the right piece of research equipment will arrive. Do not interpret this event as a sign that things are improving. It is probably a trick.

You will spend an excessive amount of time trying to get the gadget to work. Later, you will read the directions. Still later you may discover that what you really wanted all along in life was to be an English teacher. All this confusion and upset is normal, except for the part about wanting to be an English teacher.

Subproboscis—One Blind Mouse: September 21–October 20

Think about patents this month. Are your sure you haven't stumbled across something worth filing a disclosure about? Why does that super conductor you saw last week at the symphony— the one with the ceramic smile—keep popping into your mind?

Go back to your lab. Check the low-temperature electrical properties of the materials you've been studying. Remember, only *you* can file the patent application that will save us from OPEC.

Winkenus, Blinkenus, et Nodus—The Tripartite One: Thirty Days Hath September

A final report is ascendant and an audit descendant in your sphere. Take care of the final report first. It's seven months late. Get your research team together to see what's holding things up. Clue: Talk first to the graduate student who always seems to be making excuses, the one whose mother, grandfather, horse, mother, and cat died this term. See if he made a copy of the preliminary data analysis before he lined the kitty litter box with the printout after the hard disk crashed.

Pray.

Hokus Pokus—Wishful Thinker: December 1–December 24
Forget seeing your palmist this month. Your hand hasn't cracked a new line in years. If you want to find out if you got a grant, call your program officer. Before you do so, check with your grants office to see if you sent in a proposal. Writing a proposal is still one of the best ways to get a grant.

Should your grants newsletter print such a column? That's up to you. Attitudes vary on their value. One campus is wary enough to end each issue with the following notice: "Statements made in this column do not represent the official viewpoint of the campus administration. The university makes no guarantee or warranty for their accuracy."

13

Assessing Aptitude for Grants Administration

Several articles in professional journals have studied the character traits of grants administrators. One of the most provocative, published in the winter 1982 issue of the *Journal of the Society of Research Administrators* by Gerald V. Teague, H. B. Chermside, and Tammy Adelson Kirschner, used the "Cattell 16 Personality Factor Questionnaire" (16PF) to determine what kind of people make up the world of grants administration.

Unfortunately, what is a boon to the scientist can be a bane to the practitioner. The 16PF is a standardized questionnaire that has long been administered to huge populations ranging from doctors to criminals. It gathers information by asking people to report impulsively how they would think or act in a number of situations. It then groups these responses according to profession and publishes a profile against which those who take the test in the future can compare themselves to see if they would fit.

As with all such instruments, test takers are informed that there are no right or wrong answers. The first response that pops into their mind is to be considered the one most nearly true for them. So the 16PF offers innocuous statements for consideration such as:

I like to watch team games
    a. yes
    b. occasionally
    c. no
I prefer people who
    a. are reserved
    b. make friends quickly
    c. are somewhere in between a. and b.

First of all, I have a difficult time with questions for which I am assured there are no right answers. I know that if I blow enough of the ones about team games and making friends quickly, my profile could come out looking like that of a psychopath. Later, reporters would be interviewing my landlady, and a neighbor would be on TV saying, "He was such a nice man. Quiet. Always kept to himself. We never thought he'd do anything like that. What's the world coming to?"

The real problem with trying to devise the test is that the characteristics of a successful grants administrator are manifold and unique. A grantsperson should be aggressive yet subtle, creative yet realistic, financially minded yet program oriented, impatient for results yet forebearing. In myth, he is the slightly built hero who slips the bag of gold from the arms of a sleeping giant. In reality, he should work well under pressure, cry only behind closed doors, and accept a three-day deadline as no more unusual than a flea on a dog. Above all, the next one we hire should be a whole lot better than the one we are.

Because our profession is uniquely demanding, finding people who will prosper in it is difficult. We might help ourselves enormously if we took on the development of a diagnostic instrument that would test knowledge as well as character traits so that we could balance these against the puffery of a résumé or the snow job of an interview.

The instrument would begin with a few general questions:

I envy people who can walk and chew gum simultaneously
    a. often
    b. occasionally
    c. never

I increase my children's allowance
- a. annually according to the cost-of-living index
- b. whenever they reach twelve
- c. upon receipt of a satisfactory proposal justifying the increase and laying out a three-year plan for expenditures

I am most happy when I am
- a. picking a winner
- b. picking nits
- c. picking a six-pack

My short-term goals are
- a. continued employment
- b. your job
- c. chair of the board of trustees

(See what I mean about those tests having no right answers?)

A quick test for physical disabilities, such as dyslexia, that might affect the applicant's performance could be handled with a question such as the following:

Faculty consider the grants administrator
- a. a helper
- b. a lehper

Spelling and self-concept could be gauged simultaneously, especially in fat applicants, by the following:

I would wear a sweatshirt that says
- a. HUG ME
- b. HUGE ME

The inventory would then move on to explore mind-set, optimism, and general mood with such items as:

A "desert" is defined as
- a. an arid, desolate wasteland
- b. a tasty, light confection, usually spelled with two s's

Unified field theories last
  a. two nanoseconds
  b. only long enough to write down the first three of seven equations
I would read a book with the following title
  a. *The Role of the* Federal Register *in the Treatment of Insomnia*
  b. *Winning a Grant Is Never Having to Hear "I'm Sorry"*
  c. *An Introduction to Bureaucracy: The Six Dangers of Thinking Exposed*
I would take the following short course
  a. 101 Tried and True Ideas
  b. Are You in Your Right Mind?
  c. Shortcuts to Mediocrity
I would read a book entitled *Cancel All Appointments* because I think it would teach me
  a. how to manage a crisis
  b. how to leave early to go fishing
  c. how to let my whole staff go at once
You can delegate authority
  a. only if you have it in the first place
  b. and if enough administrators sign the requisition form, you can pretty much dissipate responsibility as well
Attempting to convince faculty members that indirect costs are real costs is
  a. as satisfying as petting a bald dog
  b. a modern version of the myth of Sisyphus
My best ideas for proposals occur most often
  a. to someone else
My attitude toward auditors is
  a. if I met one in a bar, I'd buy him a drink, if I didn't know he was an auditor
  b. I only hope that Hatlo really does run hell
If the program officer asks for something in writing
  a. he wasn't listening in the first place
  b. he's no good at saying "no" in person

If the foundation appointment begins on time
   a. the program officer just got some more money
   b. my watch is fast
The first thing that comes to my mind when I see NSF is
   a. the National Science Foundation
   b. a bounced check

Since a grantsperson should be resourceful, creative, and tactful, especially under adverse circumstances, we might assess these traits as follows:

"West Coast" is an anagram for "Cost Waste"
   a. true
   b. false
   c. depends on job location
Six months into a three-year project with my budget 80 percent expended and the work barely begun, I would
   a. inform the agency that the final report will be filed earlier than expected
   b. apply for full disability leave
Receiving an erroneous $275,000 duplicate payment from the National Endowment for the Arts, I would
   a. submit a revised budget with appropriate thanks
   b. apply for another driver's license in the name of Arthur Fund
Faced with two proposals of equal merit, but only one grant likely to be awarded by the foundation, I would
   a. let the foundation make up my mind
   b. rewrite both as one, emphasizing their transdisciplinary synergy
Told during an interview that our best proposal was not going to be funded, I would
   a. accuse the grants officer of cronyism and
   b. inquire discretely into how his private affair was progressing
Informed of yet another reduction in my staff, I would
   a. inadvertently leave my newly updated résumé in the photo-duplicating machine

      b. check my discretionary fund and the current rates
         for a contract out of Chicago

A few questions about knowledge of the job are in order.
We may know from the résumé that the candidate has been
writing proposals for four years, we may know from the telephone call to the present employer that this person performs
superbly, but we have no idea whether he or she knows a block
grant from a child's Christmas present. Although it would be
tacky to ask such questions in an interview, a few questions
about substantive issues folded into the instrument would hardly
be noticed among so many others. Here are some possibilities:

The following definition of a grant is most nearly accurate
    a. an alcoholic beverage
    b. an alcoholic civil war general
    c. a tranquilizer for nontenured faculty members
If the answer is "no," the question is
    a. Could you reduce the indirect costs?
    b. Could your office pick up the overrun?
    c. Will the sponsor extend the deadline?
A no-cost time extension is
    a. an extension of time on the grant with no surcharge
       to the sponsor
    b. permission to continue work with even less money
       than before
    c. inevitable
Joint funding is
    a. a bricks-and-mortar capital grant
    b. a study funded for marijuana research
    c. a grant competition for which only physical ther-
       apists are eligible
OMB is
    a. a deep sound made by an elephant
    b. a chant by Hindu mystics
    c. the initials of the Office of Mangled Budgets
A-21 is
    a. a vitamin of uncertain value

    b. an isotope emitting harmful radiation

    c. a common source of manic-depressive symptoms

An invention disclosure is

    a. loose talk in a bar

    b. a press conference held by an impulsive researcher

    c. an official form, usually filed no sooner than 366 days after publication of research results

Which definition is most accurate?

    a. principal investigator: the primary person responsible for research results

    b. principle investigator: the person who heads up an ethics committee

    c. principal investigator: the person on an ethics committee probing the actions of a local high school administrator

Which proposal title is more fundable?

    a. "The Humor of Woody Allen"

    b. "The Etiology of Humor and Other Nervous Disorders"

Gum mint is defined as

    a. a flavored chewing substance, similar to spearmint

    b. a vast bureaucracy, formerly headed by President Carter

If grants administrators acted today to perfect a diagnostic instrument such as this, it would produce

    a. the perfect grants administrator

    b. something called "Picasso's Concept of a Research Administrator."

14

Ann Granters Gets Serious

DEAR ANN: I wrote a proposal but didn't get the grant. What gives?

STILL WAITING

DEAR STILL: The directness of your letter suggests that you may have an overly simple idea of what's involved in writing a grant proposal. There's a myth that all you have to do to get a grant is write a proposal. But in fact you have to think, discuss, search, draft, trim, phone, edit, revise, amplify, consult, rewrite, polish, review, budget, send, wait, negotiate, redo, rebudget— and then you get your grant.

"Write a proposal, get a grant" is a good slogan, but that's about all. Go back over this checklist and see if maybe you haven't skipped a few steps.

$ $ $

DEAR ANN: I am ready to write a proposal for a speaker series on ethics in engineering. But the people in the grants office say it's death to use phrases like "tentatively we would like to invite." They say if I want the money, I should list the people who will come to campus, dates and all. Ann, that's why I want the money, to plan the speaker series. If I do it all in advance, there's no point in getting the grant.

REFORMER

DEAR REFORMER: I hear what you're saying, but you're going to have to do some more work. The reviewers of your proposal are not going to be impressed by the flexibility you have retained by wondering in print who you are going to invite. You should contact these people and get contingent commitments from them. Then you can write a proposal. It may not seem like fun doing all this in advance, but remember, your competition has. And if you don't, the only person besides you who will be impressed with how unfair the system is will be your mother.

$ $ $

DEAR ANN: The other day I happened to run into my dean in the coffee line at the 6-12, so I took the occasion to ask her how she would react to a request to remodel my research laboratory as cost sharing on a research grant. She gave me a noncommittal response and asked for a memorandum. I was going to send her one anyway, but I wanted some indication of whether it would be approved if I did. She gave no hints one way or the other. What gives?

COFFEE BREAK

DEAR COFFEE: Probably her patience. She may not be into curbside service. There is a myth that administrators hate paperwork and like to hear about ideas while they're buying a cup of coffee and a slice of carrot cake at the convenience store.

But deans do not become deans because they lust for the sense of power that approving requests in impromptu situations gives them. Your dean probably became an administrator because she likes building programs in an orderly, considered fashion.

The chicken crossed the street to get to the other side. Administrators often cross to get a cup of coffee. Let 'em.

$ $ $

DEAR ANN: I'm right on the verge of coming up with a set of ideas that will revolutionize research in the field of dermatology. It's a zit treatment that reduces the number of outbreaks a teenager might have. All I need are a few more positive results, but my pilot study seems to be sputtering.

The results are there, I know. I just haven't found them yet. My assistant suggested that I fudge the data we already have so we can save time. It would help me win a major grant, and the discovery would be a boon to teenagers. What do you think?

COMMITTED

DEAR COMMITTED: Resist the temptation to invent data for your research project. True, only a few more positive results will put you on the lecture circuit, but what you're planning sounds like fraud. If you're found out, the topic of your tour may be "How I Learned That Misconduct Is Not a Good Idea and That What I Really Wanted to Do Was to Teach Three Sections of Introductory Biology for the Rest of My Life."

If you're feeling punk academically, this may be a good time to update your résumé. Put in a little fluff. Add in those speeches you gave to the Kiwanis Club. List the conferences you've attended and the new courses you've developed. No harm.

But please, we don't need any more false data.

$ $ $

DEAR ANN: I want to get a grant. People keep telling me if I want one, I have to get in touch with the program officer before I write the proposal. That sounds like politics to me, and I hate politics. I should be able to write a proposal and get a grant just because I wrote a good proposal, right? This is academe, isn't it?

$99^{44}/_{100}$ THS

DEAR NINETY-NINE: You need to rethink your attitude about grants. Finding out what it takes to get one is not politics. It's just good sense. The right approach is better than the wrong approach, saying the right things is better than saying the wrong things, and putting in the right information is better than putting in the wrong information.

Remember when you were in high school and there was someone you wanted to date? Remember how many different ways you worked at finding out what would make that happen for you? Did it occur to you that that was politics? Or was it simply smart not to ask her to go bowling when what she liked was going to the movies?

Take the same attitude here. Find out beforehand as much as you can about what you should say. Treat your proposal like a love protestation. Grants are lovely things. You should have your share. Don't spend another lonely Saturday night at home while everyone else is out having fun in their laboratories just because you think normal human communication is politics.

15

Mounting an Effective Fund-a-thon

Keeping enough in the seed-grant kitty to make small awards to faculty members with promising but untested ideas is a challenge. My internal grants account has always been modest, and several attempts to persuade my boss to increase it hadn't been successful, so I decided recently to ask the research committee for some ideas. It seemed to me that a fund-raising event might help.

The committee members resisted initially. They thought fund-raising meant bake sales and most of them were on a diet. But they agreed to brainstorm for a while and not let their idea of a university interfere with their thinking.

For starters, I suggested sponsoring an answer man on TV.

"Hey, why not?" a journalism professor said gamely. "Maybe people are tired of sitcoms and want to do something about not having learned anything new since senior year.

"Picture our vice-president as emcee. Viewers tune in to the local station. She's at her office desk, we're in our classrooms or laboratories. The audience begins to call in questions."

"Good idea," said another. "Our students could prime the pump. They could ask their favorite 101 questions, like why the sky's rainbows have more colors than rainbow sherbet, or why our ears close when we yawn, or if, when we pump all the oil out of the wells, the Earth will stop spinning on its axis and grind to a halt.

"After every third answer, our VP could talk about how you can't answer questions like these without basic research and you can't have research without the venture capital of seed grants, and you can't have seed grants without donations."

"But we don't want to come across like the typical televangelist with an 800-number flashing across the bottom of the screen every few minutes," said the business school representative. "In this country, it's more blessed to watch television and *buy* something. So we should consider a deal like a commercial. Literally. Commercials are, after all, a basic part of the American fiber. We want to come across like we are too.

"Indeed, in a market economy, commercials are a public service, put there not to sell products, as many cynics assume, but to help us make better choices. And those choices, each of them, help us serve the ideals of the nation—that is, of free enterprise."

"Ah hah!" exclaimed a professor of political science. "Now I see the problem with walk-a-thons. They're completely out of line with the American character for a number of reasons.

"To begin with," he began, fishing a piece of chalk from inside his corduroy sport coat, "they aren't even American. The first -a-thon was run on foreign soil, in Greece, from Mara-something to Athens.

"Second, -a-thons don't consume enough. While people are walking, jogging, or cycling for plastic surgery for humpback whales, the only thing they're consuming is air. They may have bought a new pair of Lycra tights before they hit the track, but those things last too long to do much for the market. Until someone markets a pair that falls apart at the end of the race, it's a zero-sum cash-flow event."

"Well," drawled a classicist, scratching his stomach through an opening in his shirt, "if we want clothes that fall apart easily, I know where we find them. Take this shirt here. It's a week old and already it's going to pieces. The manufacturers must have found a new miracle fabric, like Detroit did forty years ago when it pioneered planned obsolescence. I'm sure with a little research they could improve on this shirt to make it last only one wearing."

He looked up at the ceiling. His eyes glazed over.

"I can see the ad now. A runner at the beginning of a 10K,

popping the top off a container of new tights like you open a can of new tennis balls. The air fizzes out in a spray of negative ions. The runner smiles as she shakes out the togs. 'I like Thriller's Tights.' she says. 'Great haste. Less filling.'

"Forty minutes later, she's in the shower, rinsing the remaining shreds down the drain and talking about how she loves the convenience of not having to pack sweaty clothes into her gym bag when she leaves."

The PE prof had been trying to butt into the discussion for quite a while. I recognized her.

"I was thinking of something simpler. How about maybe sponsoring a weekend football watch-a-thon. We could get people to sign up couch potatoes to pledge a nickel for each beer they guzzle and a penny for every handful of munchies they eat while they watch the games. One football weekend would earn mucho dollars for the research account, and some people would finally have the excuse they need for not leaving the living room for forty-eight hours."

"Good idea," said the business school rep, "but it doesn't hit the economy issue squarely enough. The couch potatoes would probably be eating and drinking anyway. We need something that adds to consumption."

"I've got an idea," said a professor of home economics. "Let's sponsor a shop-a-thon. People could go to May Company, Bloomingdale's, or Nieman-Marcus. In a six-hour spree, they could buy all they want and the people who sponsored them would contribute a penny for every dollar spent."

"Yeah," said the journalist, "and we could broadcast it cheap by tracking the event right through the department store surveillance cameras. All the while the buyers are spreeing, our emcee could be describing what was being bought and how much of the purchase price would go for research.

"We could even tag some of the buyers, like they do bass in a fishing contest. Then if a home viewer happened to call in to buy the same item a tagged buyer was purchasing, he or she would get the item free."

The idea caught the fancy of the committee. Within half an hour most of the details had been worked out, and a few days later I took the final proposal in to my boss.

She read it over and paused to think.

Then she reached into her desk drawer and drew out the memo I had been sending her every six months for the past three years.

"You know," she said, dropping the two-paragraph request for more seed money on the desk and pointing to it, "it has taken me a long time to see the merit of this request. What you brought in here today has opened my eyes. I'll transfer $150,000 to your seed account right away."

Fund-a-thons really work.

16

A Progression of Collectives

Biologists have coined colorful collectives to describe animals in groups. There's a pride of lions and a gaggle of geese. Others have suggested a piddle of puppies or a scratch of fleas.

The grants world deserves its own collectives which could group themselves into a roundelay that ends where it begins. Here then is a progression of collectives to suggest the endless cycle of the grants world, beginning and ending in the grasp of deadlines.

A grip of deadlines
A panic of possibilities
A fizzle of prospects
A stretch of concepts
A furrow of seed grants
A flagon of jargon
A drift of drafts
A toss of proposals
A scorn of reviewers
A yawn of committees
A spindle of turndowns
A splendor of grants
A frazzle of commitments
A garble of regulations
A bungle of bureaucrats

A slug of delays
A tedium of time extensions
A trickle of support
A clutch of auditors
A muir of paper trail
A skewer of disallowances
A dwindle of resources
A threat of memos
A grip of deadlines

17

Nightmares in the Grants Office

In the rush to review proposals at the last minute, grants administrators sometimes miss potential problems that in less stressful times they would catch in a trice. These oversights can become the stuff of nightmares, which can be of two kinds: (1) real (that is unreal—we're dealing with an oxymoron here); and (2) metaphoric (that is, the unreal real nightmare—the next thing on the day's agenda, ready to happen as soon as everything else is sufficiently out of control to make its advent inevitable).

Real nightmares happen at night while we're asleep. They put plot and character to the vague worries that dog us during the day. When we wake up, they're gone. There is no residue, no paper trail.

But when the fears of a nightmare intrude into our waking hours, we get what I call a daynag. A daynag is a nightmare that has just stepped out of the shower and is about to get dressed for work. We get the vague feeling that something is about to go wrong. A pallor falls, a drop of sweat begins at the nape of the neck and dribbles slowly down the spine to lodge at the top of the waist band.

This chapter has both a nightmare and a daynag. It begins with a real nightmare, that is, something a fellow grants administrator told me happened to her while she was in bed, with pulse slowed, and irregular darting eye movements perceptible beneath closed eyelids.

In the dream, the grants officer was in her office when the phone rang. A faculty member was calling with news that he'd just gotten his grant, worth $525,000. But he wasn't happy. He launched into a tirade about how the budget was all screwed up, how it needed to be renegotiated before he could spend the first buck, and how precious time was going to be lost.

The grants administrator was not perturbed by his upset. She knew that people have different ways of expressing their excitement about success.

"Why don't you bring the award letter up here and we'll take a look at it," she said calmly.

But as she hung up the phone, she stared out the window with that distant look of concern that benevolent chiefs on TV spy programs have whenever they've just sent their favorite agent out on a dangerous mission without any fallback plans.

She had scarcely finished her pose and pulled the file when he burst into the office.

"So what do you see as the problem?" she asked.

"The budget," he steamed. "It's all wrong."

How could it be wrong? she wondered to herself. They had had plenty of time to work it over before it went out. She had just reviewed it again, checking for all the possible routine errors: salary raise omitted? cost of living increase underestimated? travel to international symposia left out? Everything seemed fine.

"What's wrong with it?" she asked.

"The hash browns for the computer!"

"Come again?" she blinked.

Because computers were her weak area, she had always taken special pains with this part of the budget. Before a proposal went out, she would check and double check any item related to computers. This case had been no exception. Together they had discussed the line item and agreed that the entry was more than sufficient for maintenance. She did not understand his upset.

"You'll have to lead me through this slowly," she said. "We discussed that item in some detail and agreed that this amount would cover maintenance." She paused a moment, and then, hoping that some levity might help, added: "You might say we had thoroughly hashed this out."

"We had. We went over it several times. The amount would

have been fine if you had put in the right item. But you put in hash browns. This computer takes *french fries!"*

With that, the grants officer awoke, regained her normal pulse rate, and went to the kitchen for a snack, wondering whether 3:45 in the morning was too early to mosey into the office and recheck the budgets on a few recent rush proposals.

$ $ $

That nonevent was a real nightmare. It dramatized the anxiety the grants administrator had about high technology and her fear that no matter how she tried to compensate, the computer would still get her.

Daynags, on the other hand, occur while our eyes are open and we are on the payroll. They are the full-color animated version of Murphy's Law, the things psychics tell us nightmares are supposed to presage.

My favorite daynag happened more than twenty years ago at a major research university. A large, multidisciplinary, sponsored project, budgeted at close to two million in 1968 dollars, was up for renewal. Even though the deadline for the competition came up every October 1 like calendar-work, the proposal itself was always a last-minute affair, pulling everyone and everything along with it like Ma and Pa Kettle's truck packed for a move.

This year was worse than ever. The deadline had passed and the proposal wasn't finished. Three of the seven collaborating departments were still submitting material. As copy was rushed in, four typists, squeezed into an office so small they had to synchronize their carriage returns, were preparing final copy.

But the principal investigator was unruffled. He was known for his resourcefulness. His research career was said to have begun when he fished a turned-down research proposal for solid waste management out of his advisor's solid-waste containment file, rewrote it as a demonstration grant, and blew the reviewers away by printing before and after pictures on scratch-and-sniff paper.

But I digress, and this true story is beginning to take on its own dreamlike qualities. To assure you that it's true, I'll protect

the protagonist's identity by giving him a pseudonym: Bill Baylout.

The crisis was made for Baylout. He called the sponsor,
fabricated a story about a crash on the mainframe computer, and
got permission to send the proposals directly to the peer reviewers
at their home institutions, thereby saving four days and giving
the panel members the illusion that they had received all the
competitive renewals at the same time.

Then he left for his Caribbean cruise, which he had carefully
scheduled months earlier to begin the day after the deadline so
colleagues could say things like "Good job getting that proposal
off, Bill, real professional product. Now go take some time for
yourself." Baylout did.

He left behind a new administrative assistant at the project
office to manage the final typing, proofreading, printing, binding,
packaging, and mailing. No mean feat, since the proposal was
so thick each copy needed to be baled instead of stapled.

The new assistant was out to prove himself. Despite offers
from the grants development office to help, he insisted on doing
it all himself. At the end of five days of intense pressure, only
six working days after the deadline, he trundled twelve individually addressed packages off to the post office.

The next day he stopped by the research administration
office. He recounted the hectic finish, the thousands of little
decisions that Baylout hadn't left instructions for. Would sub-
sections be tabbed? Would colored paper be used for the ap-
pendixes? Would the vitas be alphabetical, chronological, grouped
according to discipline, length, pH factor? The new administrative
assistant had made all these decisions, paid his dues, earned the
privilege to hang around the sponsored programs office and gripe
about last-minute disappearing acts.

"Bet it felt good to get those packages into the mail," someone said.

"You bet," he replied. "You should have heard the postal
clerk yowl when he saw that flat of proposals roll in at 4:55
P.M.!"

" . . . not to mention the satchel full of twenty-dollar bills
to pay for the postage."

"Well, actually it didn't cost that much. Book rate is surprisingly cheap."

"Uh . . . book rate?"

"Yeah. It came to less than two dollars apiece. The total was around twenty something."

"You mailed the proposals book rate???"

And so the story came out. He had done what we all fear doing—suffered *lapsa responsibiliae* at the critical moment. As he had dollied the sealed, brown-wrapped parcels out the door of the cramped project office, a voice that had not been heard throughout the process—a sweet, motherly voice—sang out helpfully from the back of the room, "Now remember, book rate's the best way."

In those five grueling days he had asked for and accepted no help. He had made decision after decision on his own. But he was worn down. Now, a ready-made decision lofted toward him out of nowhere, and he lunged for it like a muskie. The line of his demise paid out at ten feet a second all the way to the post office.

The grants office gave him a quick course in postal rates. Within forty-eight hours a new set of twelve proposals had been reproduced, collated, bound, packaged, sealed, stamped "Please Expedite," and stickered "Special Delivery." These packages would now arrive noticeably late, only days before the review panel was to meet.

The cover letter made no mention of the other bundles bobbing their way toward each of the reviewers' mailboxes with note-in-the-bottle inevitability.

18

The Grants Administrator
as Indirect Cost

Just as the skull resting on the desk of the Medieval scholar
served as a reminder of the inevitability of death, so today's
contract administrator, ensconced in his or her cubicle, serves as
a sign to the university faculty member of the inevitability of
indirect costs.

So it is and has always been. Even though a major portion
of indirect costs on a grant or contract goes to cover expenses
for facilities, equipment, and utilities, when faculty members get
bummed about how much the indirect costs took out of their
grant, they don't gripe to their spectrophotometer, bang the heating vent, or flip off the light switch. They complain to us.

Some years ago, an incident occurred that dramatized this
bitterness. A faculty member in the English department had
finally won a grant. The journey from concept paper to sponsor
had been an arduous one, but we traveled it together and succeeded. Even though it was a humanities grant, the sponsor had
been willing to pay a portion of our normal indirect cost rate.

A few months after the grant had been awarded, I bumped
into the P.I. and his associate in the hall. Before I could ask him
how his project was going, he grabbed my tie, shoved it toward
his friend, and said, "See this tie? Nice tie, eh? My indirect costs
bought that tie!"

I was speechless. I knew faculty members resented overhead, but I had no idea about the fine detail into which they

had worked that acrimony. Not only was he angry that my salary was paid from indirect costs, but he saw this tie—this paean to autumn with its seven wood ducks flying breastward through the flack of minestrone stains—as the vile end of a vile act, an emblem of money scurrilously got, a symbol that, when examined closely, disclosed the objects themselves flocking in formation to describe a dot-to-dot scarlet letter *A* for *Avarice*.

Not all faculty members act out their rancor in such a manner. But the few who do personify the feelings many of their colleagues harbor. It's no wonder, then, that faculty member and sponsor alike seem to collude so often to leave indirect costs out of grants. Between them, they show no respect for the people caught in the middle of the grants game.

Maybe what we need is a better image for our profession. Cute people are in—dwarfs, Smurfs, elves. Why don't we promote ourselves as the helpful middlepeople of the grants world that we truly are, folks from some middleplace done in earth tones, garbed in floppy caps and loose-fitting gowns, who make things happen in the real world through our unseen ministrations?

Instead we are depicted as the Sheriff of Nottingham, exacting yet another tax, trampling on the rights of the downtrodden, riding roughshod through gardens, terrorizing children, skewering squealing pigs. It's images like these that incite faculty members to rattle pickax and lance to throw off oppressors, and their indirect costs with them.

They don't do it overtly, because we're talking about the ivory tower, and fighting like that usually takes place on the other side of the moat. Rather, they do it, appropriately enough, indirectly, usually by sending off a draft of a proposal to a sponsor with the indirect costs inadvertently left out of the budget.

Overhead left out of preliminary contact with a sponsor puts the grants officer in a tough spot. It's like a runt late for lunch. By the time it's squeezed its way to a teat, there isn't enough left to make the effort worth the while.

What bothers us is that we know, despite protestations to the contrary, that it's seldom an accident when a faculty member leaves indirect costs out of a draft proposal. But, protected as they are by the provisions of L'Accorde Genève des Academe

Internationale (the exact reference of which eludes me), the professoriate can do whatever it pleases, as long as it does so in the name of the search for Truth.

We can forget about sponsors helping us out of this fix. Convinced that there was a time—perhaps prelapsarian—when indirect costs did not exist, they continue their dogged search for the duty-free shop. Every draft they receive without indirect costs is another clue on the treasure map they hope will lead them to the mother lode of no-load research.

Why are indirect costs treated so badly?

Well, some people just don't like the term itself. To them, "indirect" connotes something devious, shifty, sneaky, like there's something going on that people are trying to hide.

Too bad. I remember the first time I learned about the concept. I was enamored with it, like Salieri when he first heard Mozart's music. Indirect costs handled an uncomfortable situation with elegance and poise. You reviewed the scope of the research project, drafted a detailed budget to cover every need of the principal investigator down to the last petri dish, and then, with a deft mathematical calculation, inserted the cost of Everything Else.

Here was an exquisite delicacy that befitted the ranks I had just joined, an intricate simplicity worthy of Mozart's finest concertos, a Zen-like quality producing a mellifluous susuration as the oil of administrative costs was poured over the turbulent waters of the direct costs below. "Off the top" put me in touch with the sublime. Indeed, shoehorning the requirements of administration in amongst the needs of the faculty would have been tacky. Like using the same locker room.

Yet despite the marvel of its conception, indirect costs don't get no respect. Faculty members seem impervious to the same wonder that moved me.

Maybe it will always be thus, but I have a dream. I have a dream that one day faculty members will learn that indirect costs are not only real costs, but costs worthy of veneration, costs to be discussed in rooms illuminated by the light filtering through stained glass windows, in places heavy with the exhalations of incense, costs to be revered before the gilded triptychs of the vice-president for research, the president, and the vice-president for business.

It can happen. The world can change. This I believe. If each person took responsibility for his or her own part of reality, he or she would be cleared in mind and heart to be open to the true meaning of research administration.

Bringing such consciousness about will not be easy. The usual grant-writing workshops that introduce faculty members to the basic concepts of budgeting and indirect costs won't do it. No, a radical approach is needed.

I propose retreats that are much closer to the original models, ones to be held in monasteries—preferably near the headquarters of the monastic order rather than at a branch office so that the concept of overhead will seem natural.

Our office would send grant winners to attend for a weekend every year. There in the quiet halls, the verdant gardens, the early morning chanting, amid the pinging of castanets and the chinging of tambourines, the concept of indirect costs could be introduced in a more palatable way. The traditional words of the most familiar chant of all—Hari Krishna—could be quietly shifted after three or four hours to "Hari Step-down, Allocation, Hari Cation, Step-down Krishna."

Later, in a lecture on the evolution of the notion of charity, the retreat master could add to discussions of love and self-sacrifice the need to pay for utilities. At the appropriate moment, the facilitator could casually mention that the origin of indirect costs has a venerable history, that the levels and rings of existence described by Dante himself in his *Divine Comedy* gave accountants at the Office of Management and Budget their first idea about how to structure the step-down method of indirect cost allocation.

A weekend in such an environment could achieve what many have failed to do with years of cautionary notes and memos—convince faculty members that overhead is as basic as dirt, and that leaving it out of a proposal is a sin against nature.

And if this failed, I might just stay at the monastery.

19

Negotiating a True Indirect Cost Rate

Indirect costs are real costs. We know that because every year or so we negotiate a rate with the federal government according to OMB Circular No. Umpteump and set one that is supposed to fit the true costs of supporting research.

But few universities consistently recover that rate after it has been set. If a sponsor lobbies long enough, a campus will lower the overhead and administer the grant just as if it had received full reimbursement.

I argue, however, that if a sponsor pays less, it should get less. The real world works that way. The little girl in the candy store with her palm full of pennies thrust upward toward the clerk asking "What can I get for this much?" is articulating the basic American question: What do you have in my price range? Real Americans don't dicker for a Snickers when all they've got money for is a lemon ball. So if there's no free munch, what keeps sponsors looking for one?

We do.

Too often, when the candy store question has been asked, we've hoisted the questioner up on the counter, told her to point to whatever she wanted, and given it to her for whatever change she had in hand.

This has to stop. We need a better answer.

I propose that we offer different classes of service, both direct and indirect, for what sponsors are willing to pay. These levels could be super, regular, and economy, depending on how much an agency has to spend. A variable overhead rate would trigger service that looks something like this:

SUPER

The "super" rate offers VIP service. (The term Pan Am uses for its premium grade—clipper class—doesn't have the right connotations.) Super calls for an indirect cost rate 50 percent higher than the negotiated one. In return, the sponsor gets the room service version of research administration. Super turns down the covers on the bed and leaves a breath mint on the pillow.

This rate offers same-day, while-you-wait, real-time research. The pace makes Captain Furillo's headquarters in "Hill Street Blues" look like the reading room of Lake Wobegon's town library. People work so fast they use the past tense to describe the blur of activity in front of them. If they're not working on today's project, it's because it was finished yesterday. There's no tomorrow.

The clocks run on metric to allow for twelve time units every working day instead of the usual eight. This way, researchers can fit in three meetings before others have calibrated their densitometer.

But even though work goes on in a supercooled frenzy, there's no pressure in the contracts room. When you're dealing with sponsors who don't ask the price of Lear jets, there's no need to get things in writing before the work begins. Contracts are all verbal. "Just get the work done and send us the bill." Pure music. New age.

Billing is handled the way you would invoice the Hope diamond. Monthly fiscal reports are preaudited and automatically discounted to reflect the average institutional audit disallowance. The vice-president for business affairs delivers the final fiscal statement at lunch, where she will simply write the number on a piece of paper and show it to the CEO, who will glance at it, nod slowly, and slip it into his coat pocket. When it comes to picking up the luncheon tab, it will be done with an ease most of us cannot muster at Taco Bell.

Researchers are the finest. Chaired professors and Nobel

Prize winners tag team to conduct the work. Facilities are *ne plus ultra*. One-of-a-kind is plural in this grammar. To say that a laboratory is state-of-the-art is to admit to playing catchup. Human subjects are the best money can buy, paid premium rates and certified as informed only after attending orientation sessions in Lausanne.

The super rate calls for super communications. Sponsors are given an 800-number, the number of the president's cellular telephone, and a hotline. Postcards travel express. The FAX machine is turbocharged.

Technical reports are printed on handmade paper, bound in leather, with titles embossed in gold. Each chapter begins with a hand-illuminated letter. The tables are Louis XIV. Couriers, handcuffed to their attaché cases, step out of the darkened recesses of stretch limousines into the blinding brightness of life to deliver reports. The executive summary is on audio tape, narrated by Walter Cronkite against a sound track of high-driving music taken from the "Halftime Highlights" segment of "Monday Night Football."

Projects are insured by Lloyd's of London to produce the results the sponsor paid for. If the original project director cannot find the answer, Blechtel (whose motto is "Results Now, Reality Later") is called in. Under its intense scrutiny, nature has never slouched. Reality yields the response the sponsors want, when they want it, where they want it.

That's super. Service now, and science too.

REGULAR

The "regular" rate is like coach on the airlines. There's less elbow room here, and no free movie. What you get is what's described in the boilerplate.

Regular service gets stuck with first-class mail. AT&T carries the phone calls. Doctoral students do the work, technical reports are stapled, fiscal reports come out at the usual pace.

Yawn.

ECONOMY

Known also as "super saver," "economy" has an indirect cost rate half that of coach, with service to match. Unlike bargain tickets on the airlines, however, there is no advance payment for this trip. Not that it wouldn't be a good idea to get the money up front from this group of sponsors. It's just that there's no sense asking. Sponsors that qualify for this rate in three essential respects—they are cheap, tight, and stingy—will not be able to scrape up the money to pay for the work before it starts.

Economy travels to the creaking of oak timbers. Meals are do-it-yourself, cooked on hibachis while miscellanea drips from the ship's ribs onto the pork fat. Entertainment is twenty minutes a day on deck for fresh air. The bonus plan is called "steerage plus."

Economy suggests a bulk-rate, coffee-break mentality disguised as old-world charm. The brochure describing this level of service has graphics of buckboards and Conestoga wagons printed in sepia tone. The environs abound with teletype, Underwood printouts, and adding machine tape.

The work pace is manyanic (muh NYAH nik; the antonym of "manic," meaning "no need to get to it today"). Its motto, mumbled every morning before work begins, is "Today Is History." The morning anthem, sung to the tune of Little Orphan Annie's "Tomorrow," goes:

The work'll come out, tomorrow,
Bet your bottom dollar that tomorrow,
We'll do some.

Just thinking about tomorrow,
Clears away the cobwebs and the sorrow,
So let's have fun.

Tomorrow, Tomorrow,
We'll work some tomorrow,
It's only a day away.

Communications are tin cans and string. Morse code is spoken. Retired railroad featherbedders find casual employment here, where they double as human subjects, especially suited for NASA-supported studies of the effects of prolonged periods of suspended animation on the human body. Informed consent is a grunt in response to the question, "So woudja wanna do sumthin' differnt 'saffernoon?'"

If a chaired professor directs a project, it's from a La-Z-Boy. Fraternities gather the research data as a community service project in exchange for the customary barrel of beer—delivered in advance. Senior citizen volunteers analyze the data, with the local National Guard unit in reserve.

The need for specialized equipment is met through a loan arrangement with the Smithsonian Institution. If measurements require precision, Coleman lanterns can be requisitioned to replace kerosene lamps.

Final reports are handwritten and stuffed into loose-leaf folders like the ones we used in third grade to carry home our spelling tests. Executive summaries follow *Reader's Digest* protocol. Where the watermark would normally occur, each page has a personalized coffee cup stain.

Fiscal administration is conducted in partitioned cubicles done in early *Daily Planet* decor. File cabinets are battleship gray. Green eyeshades filter the glare from the conical steel incandescent lamps swinging from black cords. Everyone calls the office manager "Chief."

Requests for information usually elicit an "Aw gee, lemme see now," the wire-rim glasses pushed back high on the forehead, the small finger scratching the temple, the sheer wonder of the question drawing the eyes to the ink blotter to study the fuzzy surface in a search for an answer that never quits.

Clerks run off copies of fiscal reports on a spirit duplicator and set the pages out in the sun to dry for a few weeks before mailing.

Grants administrators are trainees from a Job Corps program, on the first rung of a career ladder that begins with orienting them to the sensation of being somewhere else between nine and five other than in front of the tube and that leads a select few to a challenging career behind the counter at the post office. Those with extensive prior knowledge of game shows start out in fiscal, those versed in talk shows work with the arts and humanities, and those with film buildup from years of watching the soaps cover the social sciences. Together they promise a future that fits the hopes and wherewithal of the sponsor.

Super, regular, and economy. For once the sponsor would pay its money and get *our* choice.

20

Ask Ann Granters:
The Movie

DEAR ANN: I sent out a proposal the other day without getting the university's permission. I know I shouldn't have, but I'm in the liberal arts, and it's hard to get grants here. Humanities sponsors don't pay much indirect costs, and the people in the grants office are real sticklers for it. So I thought I better wait till I got the grant to tell them about the proposal.

AN HISTORIAN

DEAR AN: I'm partial to people with the same first name as mine, though I'm not familiar with that spelling. Is it Swedish?

You seem to believe in the new adage that it's easier to win forgiveness than to get permission. That saying is about as accurate as the one that says a person with a liberal arts degree can get a job in just about any field he or she wants. Keep up what you're doing and you may find out that neither adage is particularly true.

$ $ $

DEAR ANN: A friend of mine has an unusual problem. She (not her real pronoun) is a department chair and has been approached by an aerospace company that's in trouble with the federal government. The company has been dinged for lousy paperwork and needs to demonstrate its ability to spend money responsibly before it can get another major contract.

Our campus doesn't get many grants, but when it does, it's great at following federal regulations. So the company wants our campus to be the prime contractor on its next proposal, with the bulk of the work subcontracted to them, so we can help them rebuild their credibility. The company is also proposing something that neither the department chair nor I have heard before. It says our overhead rate of 68 percent total direct costs is okay, but that the faculty's salaries are too high and will kill the project. It wants us to cut them in half.

The deliverables are a three-page technical report and a dumpster full of memos, requisitions, and change orders.

The department chair has tried to find researchers who will take on the project but has had no luck. Faculty members won't believe the company can't afford their salaries. What should she do?

BOLLIXED

DEAR BOL: You and she can start by stopping the phony letters. I'm sick of getting junk like this written by administrators who are trying to trivialize the serious problems professors face. Don't waste my time. I've got real problems to deal with, as the following letter shows.

$ $ $

DEAR ANN: I want to get a grant from the Exwhyzee Company but can't because the overhead at our campus is way out of line.

Exwhyzee is small. It can't afford to pay for laboratories that are already there and the exorbitant salaries of our grants administrators. Our indirect cost rate is 55 percent of salaries and wages. Can't the university drop it just for this one deal? It'll never notice another grant.

BEING FLEECED

DEAR BEING: I hear what you're saying. Those administrators earn enormous salaries, and, what's worse, they will hardly notice your grant once it comes in. You'll realize this as soon as the dean passes you in the hall and doesn't mention it.

Try asking them to cut the rate. If they refuse, here's a clever way you can do it without their permission. Drop your own salary to a third of what you want. Then the administrators will have to cut the overhead to match, since it's tied to salaries. You'll be taking dollars right out of their pocket, and since it's entirely legal, they can't do a thing about it. Slick, eh?

$ $ $

DEAR ANN: Recently I had an overrun on a contract. We were designing a piece of equipment, a prototype, for a company and things got a little out of hand. I added a few too many refinements and the final product cost 25 percent more than what we had budgeted. The sponsor won't pay for the extras.

I'm in deep trouble. My department head is so honked he's threatening to read my next proposal before he signs it.

SCARED

DEAR SCARED: You're describing a common phenomenon. Some faculty members believe that even though an industrial sponsor ordered a moped, it secretly wants a full-dress Harley. So they do a super job on the assumption that a superior product will move the sponsor after the fact to pay for the extras—bells, whistles, and all.

Unfortunately, industry wants just what it paid for. It has little imagination. If it did have some, it would be on the faculty.

Next time, just follow the directions and avoid excessive use.

$ $ $

DEAR ANN: I've got a problem. The Human Subjects Committee on our campus says that we can't do deception studies whenever we want to. But I'm on the verge of landing a contract to explore Allen Funt's lasting impact on America. A sponsor wants to find out how our trust in the verisimilitude of daily events has changed since "Candid Camera" hit the scene. Just last week, for instance, when a mugging, a convenience store robbery, and a four-car pileup occurred in the space of three minutes, a witness turned and asked a stoplight, "Am I on Candid Camera?"

I drafted a study to see if people would undress in front of a person who had "Phony Doctor" printed on his T-shirt, or whether they would turn and ask the "Candid Camera" question. But the yahoos on the Human Subjects Committee turned down the research protocol. They said that what we might learn was not as important as the potential damage we might cause the subjects by continuing to deceive them.

Ann, the committee reads your column all the time. Please tell them they're wrong.

SINCERE SEEKER

DEAR SINC: Look here, toots, the world is uncertain enough without having a bunch of people going around playing grammar school tricks like hiding video camcorders and then publishing the results. Every time you do something like this, you reduce the public's credibility level a lot more than Allen Funt ever did. The committee did the right thing.

By the way, did you know that a famous Midwest social research institute won a twenty-year contract for a longitudinal triple-blind study of people who are addicted to doing deception studies? It's trying to find out what makes people want to learn about human nature this way. The work is in its twelfth year now.

No one knows who's in the experimental cohort. I wonder if you are.

$ $ $

DEAR ANN: I'm in a quandary. I know one of the important new directions in research involves my working outside the department with a new interdisciplinary institute. The old guard in the department says I should stick with research in my discipline. What do you think?

EXCITED

DEAR EXCITED: It's okay to consult on a research grant or two through an interdisciplinary institute, but until you are a full professor, be careful about spending too much time outside the department.

Getting involved in interdisciplinary research is a lot like having an affair. The experience is exciting and exhilarating. You feel like you're extending your inner self, stretching your horizons, pushing yourself to limits you hadn't experienced before.

But your departmental colleagues are likely to be suspicious of your newfound enthusiasm and to act jealous. They'll insinuate that the work of the institute is flashy, superficial, that its researchers are publicity mongers. They'll accuse you of acting like you're too good for the rest of the department and of having forgotten who gave you tenure. They'll complain that you're neglecting your students, exposing them to suspect ideas, and assigning them spurious dissertation topics that might ruin their chances for a reputable career.

So be careful. Consult on an occasional grant at the institute, but remember where your roots are. Don't let the seductive glamour of the interdisciplinary turn your head—at least not until you're a full professor.

$ $ $

DEAR ANN: I was just hired on my first job at a prestigious private institution on the West Coast and am ready to write a few proposals. I went to the grants office to get some details on budgets. Whenever I asked about the indirect cost rate, they changed the topic. What gives?

PERPLEXED

DEAR PERPLEXED: I assume that you're writing from the institution whose name appears in the embossed letters of the return address on your envelope. Sorry, but if you have to ask what their indirect cost rate is, you can't afford it.

21

Budgeting Tips: L'Eggacie de la Duc d'Or

By now we've all attended the workshops and read the books by the experts who tell us how to write great grants. We've listened, taken notes, studied. And most of us are still waiting for the money to roll in. What's taking so long? How is it that the experts can divulge their secrets and still outstrip us, winning grants at a rate of ten of theirs to every one of ours? Are their books and workshops just a scam to tantalize us with riches but make only them rich?

To find out, I decided to investigate one of the most famous grant-winning duos, Bodek and Blauer. This East Coast act is known for its seminars on grants development and celebrated for its book on budgeting: *Don't Budget, Fudge It!*

But arranging for an interview was harder than I had expected. I wrote three letters and placed four phone calls. All went unanswered.

I was about to give up when a friend at the State Department got me on track. She told me about a group called Imnasty International, a worldwide organization known for its ability to locate the elusive. I contacted them.

I was in luck. It turned out that Imnasty not only knew about Bodek and Blauer but was collaborating with them at that moment on a proposal that was in its final stages. Imnasty would soon be taking them a revised draft for final touches. I was invited to go along when they delivered it. Indeed, they asked, would I mind dropping it off for them?

"Sure," I said. "Why not." They set a time.

I was helicoptered to the Crank and Thank Tank where, Imnasty told me, Bodek and Blauer did most of their work. The tank is a combination health spa–proposal-writing retreat buried deep in the Appalachians. I wondered how they buried it in their indirect cost rate as well.

I was ushered into a large room set up for the conference. Bodek and Blauer were already there. At least I think it was them. Under the conditions of the interview their faces were in shadows, obscured by heavy backlighting. They spoke through microphones that altered their voices. One sounded like Bogart, the other like Donald Duck. My microphone made me sound like Barbara Walters.

I had only thirty minutes for the interview. I decided not to waste time on pointless questions about secrecy.

"What do you do," I began, "in a situation where a sponsor is a little short of what my son calls 'flow'? When it doesn't have all the cash you need to run a project?"

"First of all, shon," said the Bogart sound-alike, "you got our book all wrong. We wrote about how to shave bucks once you get a grant, not how to write cheap proposals."

I knew that I should have read the book. I scrambled to recover.

"Of course," I said, "any teaching assistant knows that. But didn't I hear somewhere that you're writing a book on proposal budgeting too?"

I had gotten lucky. They shifted in their seats, even seemed to squirm. Then they put their heads together and whispered. Their voices whined high like a tape recorder played fast. Then composure followed.

"Why yes," the duck began, taking out a penknife and sharpening a quill. "We're glad you asked. We do have a few ideas from our new book we'd be glad to share with you.

"We try to work with people who want to live within their budgets. 'Grant now, pay later,' 'Ninety days same as cash,' '8.8 percent financing'—that sort of thing.

"And we even run specials. Instant $5,000 rebates for every $100,000 in—"

"Wait a minute," Bogie interrupted. "The duck's too shoft on these wimps. I don't feel shorry for 'em. I panic the suckers. I tell 'em a cost-of-living increase is coming, but I'll hold the prices steady for six months if they'll make an award now. Then when the bill comes due, I hit 'em with a carrying charge and an interest rate of 21 percent."

"Isn't that a little high these days?" I asked.

"Sho what? They've got money you can't imagine. If they won't bite on the six-month come-on, I offer to lease 'em research. I give 'em the action for a couple of years at a ridiculously low monthly payment. Then, when they want the final report, I grin and show 'em the four-point type where it says it'll run 'em about 80 percent of the original budget. They can't wiggle out of it then. I've got 'em by the short h—" He stopped, glanced at his partner, and resumed, ". . . by the down."

I frowned. I knew I wasn't getting the real story but I didn't know why. Were they just too sly to give out the best answers in an interview?

"My partner tends to overstate things," the duck said calmly, resuming its thread of thought. "Why don't we share with you some of the new things we've been trying.

"Right now, for instance, we're negotiating a new research laboratory with the National Science Foundation. But since the foundation can't pick up the total cost of a new building, we're negotiating with the Department of Defense to carry back a second on a grantage with very flexible terms."

"A grantage?" I blinked.

"It's like a mortgage," explained the duck. "Gives DOD a chance to pick up some extra cash on bucks it's got lying around. They've even offered us a fixed-rate agreement."

The interview went on like that. I was being jerked around. I could feel it. I tried a few more topics with the same results and was just about to launch into questions about overhead when my watch beeped.

The thirty minutes were up. I thanked my hosts and left the great hall. I stepped out into the sunlight and strolled down the curved driveway past marble statues of Greek goddesses.

When I reached the bottom, I turned back to gaze one last time at the villa through the spray of a huge fountain. I was absent-mindedly cleaning my ear when I realized the whopping in my head was the sound of helicopter rotors. I looked up to see the Imnasty pilot frantically signaling me to grab the rope ladder.

I latched on. The copter lurched. Within moments I was swept through the topmost jet of the fountain into the craft's cockpit. As I settled into my seat and wrung out my pants legs, the pilot asked me if I'd remembered to leave the proposal package behind.

"Yes," I shouted. "I left the attaché case next to the coffee table, just like you said."

"Good," he shouted back. The copter dropped over a ridge, leaving the scene behind. It lurched, as though it had hit a large air pocket. Then it settled down and took off. In the rear view mirror I caught a glimpse of what looked like an early red sunset.

Back in the office I checked in with Margaret. She had been doing some investigative research of her own.

"Whatcha got?" I asked.

"Real curious," she said. "Two possibilities."

"Shoot." I said. I had always wanted to say that.

The first bullet came uncomfortably close. She had always wanted to do that.

"No," I said, "I mean give me the report."

"Oh," she said. "Well, one source claims that Bodek and Blauer are on an insider's list of the habitually frugal and compulsively competent. It seems Washington keeps a list of 'best buy' research institutions. If you're on it, all your proposals have an automatic edge over everyone else's. The final technical score is increased 25 percent, and the cost proposal is decreased by 25 percent before it's compared to other bids, then restored to normal if you win."

"Can we get on it?" I asked.

"Nah. It's like the MacArthur Foundation genius grants. You can't apply. You're either on it or you're not."

"Interesting," I said. "What's the other deal?"

"This one's wild. My other source claims that B & B are getting rich on a little-known federal loophole. They're supposedly one of the last campuses covered by the Sand Lot Act of 1968.

"The Sand Lot Act? What's that?"

"It was an attempt to help urban colleges that were lagging behind everyone else catch up. Under it, protected institutions request government assistance in constant 1968 dollars. Once the program people buy off on the technical part of the grant, if the grantee institution is on the list, the contracting officer ships it over to the Federal Reserve where it's adjusted to compensate for over twenty years of inflation. That equals a factor of 4.2. The Treasury Department prints the extra dollars, the agency lives within its budget, and instead of $100,000 B & B get a grant for $420,000. Pretty slick, eh?"

"Just how many of these sand lot colleges are there?" I asked.

"There used to be quite a few," Margaret replied, "but the present administration got wind of the deal a few years ago and has been shutting them down one by one. They're the final vestige of the Great Society to be dismantled. Washington is eager to clean up the last few, but there's no clue as to how they're going to do it."

Suddenly the frantic exit, the shock wave, the red sky— even what I had dismissed earlier as a Middle East affectation in the punctuation of the lettering on the side of the helicopter— I'MNASTY—made sense.

There was more than a peanut butter sandwich and a banana in the briefcase I had left behind. A lame-duck administration was having its last quack. I had been the dupe of a snuff group.

I slumped back in my seat.

Now, I thought, I'll never find out how they hid the cost of that spa in their indirect cost base.

22

Playing Hardball on Lowball: An Affordable Future

The temptation to lowball on contract quotations is strong. The federal government has been plagued by companies that submit purposely low bids for contracts so they can win the job and then recover hidden costs through a carefully orchestrated symphony of change orders. Among the worst offenders are companies that contract with the Department of Defense (DOD), where stories about fifty-dollar screws are prolific.

Figures show that the typical DOD overrun is more a marathon than a fun run. The average contractor jogs about 270 percent over estimate. The mark for industry was set by one contractor that regularly staggered 480 percent over original projections. (For its accomplishment, it was decorated in *The Jack Anderson Book of Federal Records,* the best-seller published with all its numbers expressed in exponentials to keep it to one volume.)

But the day of the lowball is going the way of pinball. The Office of Management and Budget (OMB) is experimenting with ways to control such ruses. I called up a friend there to get some details.

"What's the story about cost control at DOD?"

"It's in."

"I know that. But what about this new approach to controlling lowballs?"

"It was my idea. I got the brainstorm a few months ago while I was bowling."

"You bowl?"

"Yeah. With the prospect of the administration turning Democratic in the next election, most of us in the agencies are working on our averages again. Believe me, budget hearings go a whole lot smoother when you casually pull back your sport coat and the Democrats on the committee see your nickname embroidered above your shirt pocket.

"Well, there I was, sitting at the bowling alley one night, entering the team handicaps on the score sheet, when it clobbered me that we ought to do something like that with bids from defense contractors."

"Why?" I asked.

"Let's face it. Corporate nature being what it is, when a company sends in a bid for a new weapons system, it's bound to underestimate how much it's going to cost so it can get the contract. For defense contractors especially, budgeting is the art of defining the future the way Congress wants to see it—as affordable. If you can't make your bid look like you're giving them a BMW for the price of an Escort, you're out of luck. So contractors hedge."

"Okay, but how hard is it to detect a lowball?"

"It varies. Some lowballs are easy to pick out. Take a $720 bid for a coffee pot. Even a novice contracting officer can spot that lowball. Accept that sucker, and you'd be in for two or three sure contract modifications—and a trip to the carpet to explain to your boss how you missed the smoke and mirrors in that cost proposal. But most of the stuff is a lot more subtle than that."

"So how do you plan to control it?"

"Well, I said that we should start by accepting the lowball as inevitable. Then we should figure in a factor for each contractor the way we do a handicap for each bowling team to make the evening's competition more interesting.

"Once the brass bought that, the rest was easy. What we do now is calculate the average overrun on the last ten projects for each defense contractor. Then we apply that factor to the budget of each new proposal to project the probable final cost. It's given a whole new sense to the term 'adjusted gross.' "

"I'll tell my secretary," I said. "She thinks 'adjusted gross' means the final draft of something I've written. Go on."

"Here's the next step. We take a budget figure from the cost proposal, like $10,000,000, and modify it to accommodate the average overrun for a company—say 220 percent—to arrive at an adjusted bid of $32,000,000. Once we've reworked all the bids, we use these figures to compare them, and we award the contract to the outfit that sent in the best adjusted lowball."

"Adjusted lowball? That sounds like a term from psychotherapy."

"It's a little like that. We see this as corporate reality rehabilitation."

"Well, what about the company that doesn't have a track record yet? How do you handle it?"

"We've allowed for that. We load all newcomers' bids with three-fourths of the average overrun until they establish their own handicap."

"Your idea sounds great," I said, "but I hear the generals and admirals are the real problem. They keep adding bells and whistles to projects until they make a cuckoo clock sound like the campanile at St. Mark's."

"That's covered. Remember, everyone's got to satisfy the same users. The company that consistently controls the generals' desires to enhance and enhance will eventually bring its handicap down and get the competitive edge."

"Do you see any problems yet with your plan?"

"Yep, and unfortunately it's a big one. Once Congress sees that the bidders' pricing practices are more like Neiman-Marcus than Pic-N-Save, the future may no longer be affordable. We might not see a new weapons system for years."

This could present some problems, I thought. I said goodbye and called an acquaintance of mine at a defense contractor to see how she saw it.

"We're cautiously optimistic about OMB's proposal," she said. "Corporate thinks we can work with it."

"How's that?" I asked.

"We've plans to take a proactive approach and use the system to our advantage. Our first step will be to design and build three or four fighters and some bombers at cost."

"Why?"

"We want to build up our handicap for a killing. There's a rumor about a juicy new contract at NASA. We want it."

"What's that?"

"It's one for a new toilet seat."

23

Answering Questionnaires; or, Would You Mind Not Repeating That Question?

Recently, I went through a surprisingly productive period. In five weeks I drafted three proposals, edited four more, revised the proposal approval form, completed a guide to project budgeting, and rewrote the university's policy on consulting.

For a while I attributed that prodigious output to the fact that it was summer, the faculty was away, and there was time for more than crisis handling. But that didn't seem right. Other summers had come and gone with my fond hopes for catching up unrealized.

Maybe it was the resumption of yoga. I could feel energy surging from my inner being, like the rays of light emanating from the forehead and abdomen of the yogis pictured on the front covers of how-to books in the occult sections of bookstores.

But that answer also seemed too pat.

Then it struck me: I hadn't received a mail survey in over a month.

No wonder life seemed inexplicably rewarding.

Why is it that a questionnaire has the power to destroy the equanimity of an otherwise manageably hectic existence? It usually isn't too demanding, but it might as well be a telegram with news of personal disaster for all the havoc it wreaks. From the initial "Dear Colleague" to the inevitable "We will be happy to send you a copy of the results" (have you ever gotten yours?), its arrival is a banana peel under the insole of my daily routine.

Generally I deal with questionnaires the way I suppose everyone else does. As soon as one arrives, I slip it to the bottom of my stack of mail. When it emerges again, I scan a few lines and slide it onto my left-hand pile. Like the last pea on a dinner plate with no mashed potatoes to keep it from traveling round and round, the questionnaire moves from pile to pile until finally I exercise Survey Handling Strategy A. That calls for referring the questionnaire to another office.

But Strategy A seldom works, and since there is no Strategy B, when the questionnaire comes back with a note saying, "I think your office is the one best equipped to handle this," I have no choice but to begin to answer the survey.

As soon as I start to answer, I stop again. I wonder for what kind of university this questionnaire was devised. Usually it fits our campus like a caftan fits a parrot. The statistical data requested are items that I never thought to collect. All multiple-choice questions drive me to "other."

I consider guessing, but an auditor might later disallow $800,000 of a $600,000 program because the numbers reported here vary from other data. By the time I'm half through, the survey has impugned my control over the organization of my office and undermined my sense of what's important and what's trivial.

That quandary escalated over the years with the arrival of each questionnaire. But fortunately that has all changed now, thanks to the serendipitous effect of a system I devised to help control the mechanics of answering surveys.

A while ago I decided to set up a file called "Miscellaneous Reports and Questionnaires," where I put a copy of every questionnaire I ever filled out and every report I ever wrote.

In less than a year the file was two inches thick. Then, whenever a questionnaire arrived, I would look there to find most of the information I needed for the survey. Filling out questionnaires soon took half the time it used to.

The system was useful, but I had no idea it would set me free.

Liberation happened about eighteen months after I devised

the system. The dean of our School of Business had activated Strategy A by sending me a survey he'd received from a fellow dean at Whatsup U, asking me to fill in the blanks.

The form asked a series of questions about how we handled indirect costs internally. It was prefaced with a cover letter which had a capacious apology that set an indoor record. The writer was abject about sending out this inquiry. "We are all deluged with such requests," he acknowledged, but there was simply no way he could get this important information without bothering us with a questionnaire.

The questionnaire was not too long—three pages—with the usual questions. But as I went through them, they sounded a bit *too* usual. My suspicions were aroused. I sorted quickly through the top items in my questionnaire-survival file and found a copy of the same questionnaire I had filled out two months earlier. The same survey had been sent to me by our dean of engineering after he had received it from the dean of engineering at, once again, Whatsup U.

Apparently, Whatsup's business dean had seen what the engineering dean had done and saw an opportunity for an easy report to his school on how other business schools handled their indirect costs. So he had it retyped and sent out.

He hadn't planned, of course, on both questionnaires being referred to the same place as soon as they arrived on a campus.

When I realized what had happened, I was quickly cured of ever again considering survey authors serious researchers. In my heart I had always known that 99 percent of the questionnaires mailed wouldn't produce a valid truth if the Buddha had hand-delivered the answers, but I had paid homage to the search anyway.

Now I saw the light. Questionnaire framers are just like you and me. They are people who like to get mail—something better than junk mail, but nothing too personal. It's like when I was in fifth grade and found out that for forty-eight cents I could send a postcard to every secretary of state in the country, ask for information, and for weeks afterward have my mailbox stuffed with maps, brochures, and flyers. I recall feeling important for the first time in my life as mail arrived daily with my name on it.

With that insight, I began to approach questionnaires differently. Now I return them promptly. I give information that is about 40 percent accurate (gathered from my Q & R file) and 60 percent estimate. I even change some of the data that haven't changed just to give the impression of recently adjusted, up-to-date information.

There's only one problem. Now that I know that questionnaire writers are lonely souls reaching out in their own dim way to communicate, I find myself lingering much longer over the inevitable last question—the open-ended one that asks if there's anything I can add to make their search more meaningful.

24

Golden Fleece Awards: The Politics of Negative Results

Senator William Proxmire of Wisconsin, a grants watcher for many years, has bestowed a long series of Golden Fleece Awards. These awards honor grant recipients who, he claims, have shorn the public of its tax dollars by pursuing naïve or unnecessary studies.

In recent years, the senator's staff seems to have dozed and missed some contracts worthy of at least a silver or a bronze as examples of projects that have bilked the public. The oversights of his staff are even more surprising in view of the fact that the results of these studies were widely disseminated in such thought-provoking weeklies as *The Subway Strap Hanger's Digest* and the *Counterintuitive Review.*

I nominate the following for the consideration of the senator:

National Geographic: The Doomsday Machine Revisited

The famous report on "National Geographic: The Doomsday Machine" first appeared in the *Journal of Irreproducible Results* in 1974. Despite the convincing design of the research, the careful execution of its methodology, and the irrefutable results of the original study, the U.S. Department of Interior insisted on spending yet another $782,000 on three separate follow-ups to verify the original projections.

For these taxpayer dollars, the department learned that the original projections were off by only 3 percent. At the current rate of accumulation, it would take 173, not 168, years for the absolute weight of the *National Geographics* stored in garages, attics, and basements to trigger major seismic events, accelerate the sinking of mining towns, and add enough mass to cause ocean-cliff homes to seek equilibrium in the surf.

A lot of money was spent. All the taxpayer got was a minor adjustment in projections and a five-year delay in the appointment of charter members to the President's Commission on the Prospect of National Destruction by Forces Other Than Communistic.

A Secure Future for Social Security

Investigators at the Institute on Social Comport spent $1,889,000 of the taxpayer's money on "A Secure Future," a boondoggle that started as a limited study but ended up chasing down every option for ensuring the survival of the social security system. The institute overspent the original budget of $129,000 by approximately 1,364 percent. Its researchers filed a record eighteen requests for cost augmentations.

As each potential solution was considered, it was immediately discarded as hopeless until, finally, the study lodged on one promising possibility: vanity social security numbers.

The researchers reasoned that citizens might pay an additional twenty-five dollars a year—just as they do for vanity license plates on automobiles—to express their individuality every time they applied for a loan, cashed a check, or borrowed a library book, and thereby save the social security system.

Phrases that were expected to go quickly were: "WHT ME WRRY," "NOT MY NAME," and "HVE NCE DAY."

Life-Cycle Costing of Selected Careers

This study, supported by the Department of Labor, explored the cost/benefit ratio of forty-eight of society's most common professions. To identify the ideal profession, the study took into account all the elements of a career, not simply salary. It examined the cost of required education and time involved, lost earnings while pursuing that education, internship requirements, the capital investment necessary to start a practice, the overhead in running the business, probability of success, tax shelter possibilities, stress and health effects, and impact on family life.

When all quality-of-life and cost elements were factored in, one career emerged with a clear edge: bank robbery.

These results were corroborated by another study that reported that the average bank robber is apprehended during his or her eighteenth heist. Given that the risk of arrest increases geometrically with each job, the likelihood of being caught during the first three capers is quite small, only .03. Compared to the failure rate of new franchises (.13), new small businesses (.27), and new restaurants (.64), the cost/benefit ratio of bank robbery is appealing indeed.

Since the risk of failure is so small on the first three tries, one does not have to be highly trained to succeed. Indeed, in an uncharacteristic lapse of professionalism, the Department of Labor suggested that those who wish to pursue this profession should go for the big ones on the first two tries and plan on retiring after the third.

What makes robbing banks even more desirable as a career is that it is insured by an organization as reliable as the FDIC. If you fail, the government automatically picks up all living expenses until you're ready to try again.

The Gravity of Legislative Compliance

Hidden behind this trendy title was a contract for $642,000 issued by the Department of Health and Human Services (DHHS) to see if it could control the operation of the law of gravity in those states that fail to comply with Title IX legislation.

The contract resulted from a remark made by a Professor Blake at a plenary session of the Forty-seventh Annual Conference of the Society on the Redundancy of History. Society members, not buffaloed by Santayana's dictum that those ignorant of history are doomed to repeat it, believe that it is inevitable that the events of history will recur. The society's goal is to uncover the quasi-scientific rules that govern the penchant of the present to give the past a second, third, and even a fourth chance.

Professor Blake was answering questions about his keynote address when a member of the society rose to ask him just how much history had to repeat itself before the society would verify that a scientific principle had been demonstrated. Sensing a trap, Blake employed Socrates's escape: he answered the question with a question.

"You ask your question as if the principles of the so-called hard sciences are something we should use as our measure of success," he began. "But let's examine the assumptions of physical science. How do we know that our 'physical' principles aren't themselves just historical events, treated like laws because they repeat themselves so often?

"Can we, for instance, really have confidence in the law of gravity? After all, no one has isolated the gravitational force in any particle of matter. We have only statistical evidence for its presence. Its operation might simply be a phenomenal series of coincidences helped along by a public that believes in its existence because it is convenient for the survival of commerce and industry."

Members of the audience stopped coughing and started listening. Blake went on to point out that there may already be evidence that gravity is giving in. As some people have begun to question its power, he said, others are becoming less self-conscious about reporting such things as levitation.

"Floating in space is coming out of the closet. Occurrences are now being reported with such regularity that scientists are beginning to wonder whether levitation has always been this common, or whether the so-called law of gravity itself is beginning to break down, a latent victim of the questioning of traditional values begun in the early '60s."

The DHHS latched on to the offhand remark. It reasoned that if the law of gravity is not immutable, it may be controllable. The toes of the DHHS secretary twinkled as he dreamed of the power that authority over gravity would give him. He envisioned himself able to command the very flow of the waters that passed beneath a bridge. Just by cutting the force of gravity a third, he could send a warning signal to universities and colleges that sex discrimination would no longer be tolerated. Waters would slosh freely over river banks. Stream and riverbed would seem no more related to each other than balloons unfettered on an open barge.

Here was the leverage DHHS needed to force compliance with regulations about equal access and affirmative action. It rushed to fund a study and got one of the heaviest lightweights in the gravitation business to direct it.

Initial progress reports were promising: it looked like Blake's musings had substance. Major errors in assumptions had been made in the equations used to explain gravity.

Then the reports stopped. No sooner were things beginning to look good for governing gravity than phone calls to the project director for more details went ignored, and FAXes went unacknowledged. Months passed while DHHS officials waited anxiously for word.

Stories began to circulate that the project director himself had disappeared. They were soon confirmed. He was never located. No final report was ever filed.

The study ended in disappointment. Over $3.6 million was spent with no results except for rumors that somewhere someone was filling a warehouse full of shoes with Velcro soles.

25

Peer Review: Knowing When to Say No

Peer review of proposals can be rough. I worked on a panel once that was quite hard on proposals with budgets that looked padded. After two days of cutting here and trimming there, the committee came across one proposal whose budget was particularly overstated. It responded mercilessly, slashing student assistance, cutting travel, pruning materials and supplies. Still its lust to cut was not sated. When it came to the final item in the budget—"Other"—the chair of the panel roared: "Look at that, $500 for 'Other!' That's absurd. I can get 'Other' for half that."

Like democracy, the peer review system is the worst method of determining scientific merit—except for all the others. There is no question but that sometimes the biases of reviewers interfere with their thinking about programmatic features. The likelihood of this happening is heightened (1) if a proposal's idea is sweeping in scope, (2) if it challenges established theories in the field, and (3) if it comes from a campus off the beaten research track.

Normally, no one sees the review. Peers read research proposals in the quiet of their study and mail their results to the program officer who reports them anonymously to the author.

Recently, however, I witnessed an impromptu review in Vancouver. I had stepped into the bar of the same hotel where the annual meeting of the American Psychological Association was convened. The early afternoon session had just adjourned, and the participants who were not going to the late afternoon session on drug dependency were filing into the cocktail lounge.

On the stools to my right were two conferees. They had just discovered that each had received the same research proposal for review. It was at my elbow, opened to the first page.

Written for the National Institute for Mental Health, the proposal was from an obscure university near the Canadian border—Forgette U, as I recall—and offered a thesis that would test the open-mindedness of a lot of professionals. The rationale, as explained on the first page, went something like this:

> Guilt is the only true human emotion. All other emotions—sadness, happiness, fear, anger—are learned.
>
> This hypothesis is readily demonstrable. When a baby smiles, its parents smile, when a baby cries, they comfort it. The manifestations of happiness and sadness are easily observed by the parents and can therefore be easily reinforced. As a result, these behaviors persist. Because they are learned so early, they seem genetic.
>
> In contrast, the manifestations of guilt are not physically observable in infants. Children must be able to speak in order for us to know that they are feeling guilty. Therefore, parents cannot reinforce guilt in children until they can talk, which normally occurs when they reach the age of two. Until then, parents can reinforce guilt only randomly. For guilt to appear to be so well learned, as it does, and to persist almost intact into adulthood, it cannot have been acquired. It must be genetic.

I came in at the beginning of the conversation:

SHE: So guilt is in the DNA, eh? Can you believe this tripe?

HE: Right back to the Middle Ages. If what he says is true, we could replace psychologists with genetic engineers.

SHE: I wonder what he thinks we should do with Margaret Mead's work? The Samoans don't lay guilt trips on their kids, and they grow up well adjusted. I suppose he'd say the whole Samoan culture is genetically deficient, like a tribe of emotional albinos.

HE: I guess. He really believes that it's unnatural for people to have sex, leave kids with babysitters, and pay mechanics to repair their cars without experiencing guilt. I think he's going to honk a lot of people off by accusing them of being—what does he call them—"guiltual psychopaths"—just because they aren't swimming in guilt.

SHE: Why didn't he footnote that term?

HE: I think because he invented it. But, you know, the more I think about those people—and I'm speaking now as a private individual, not as a professional— the more I wonder. Haven't you ever puzzled about the ones who say they don't feel guilt? They can leave the toilet seat up with no more remorse than others have about forgetting the date of the Treaty of Versailles.

SHE: 1783, wasn't it?

HE: That's not important right now—I think it was 1919— the point is, I'm worrying about dismissing this thesis too casually just because it makes me feel uneasy.

SHE: Huh?

HE: Well, I think we should look at his claim. Like he says, we know that human genes can be affected by radiation. And that people in the Sunbelt seem more free of guilt than those in the Cloudbelt. Could it be that solar radiation breaks down the guilt mechanism in genes? Maybe guilt can be treated with radiation therapy, much like cancer?

SHE: (laughing) You mean that the counterculture types who fled west to obliterate their guilt with pot were really being cooked by the radiation leaking out of their solar collectors?

HE: Maybe.

SHE: Wait a minute. It's beginning to sound like you're giving this malarkey some credence.

HE: Well, let's just suppose there is a shred of truth here, okay? The author claims that joy is learned and guilt is genetic, right?

SHE: Right.

HE: Well, isn't it true that one trauma often destroys joy permanently?

'SHE: Yes.

HE: But have you ever heard of a single trauma knocking out guilt forever?

SHE: No.

HE: Or even eight years of psychotherapy finishing it off permanently?

SHE: Be careful now. You're toying with our bread and butter.

HE: And don't we sometimes blame religions as the producers and perpetuators of guilt?

SHE: Yes.

HE: But have any of the great masters ever said anything in their teachings about guilt?

SHE: Not much.

HE: And yet their followers dwell on it, almost as if there were something non-eradicable in human nature that needed to be explained?

SHE: You mean, like, since it's already there, you don't have to produce it, just explain it?

HE: Exactly.

SHE: Okay, let's say he's right. That still wouldn't change my mind about this proposal. I would never recommend it for funding.

HE: Why not?

SHE: Because if I did, Proxmire might get hold of it and use it to make our discipline look ridiculous.

HE: And?

SHE: I'd feel guilty.

I have always been a strong supporter of research in psychology. But that scene worried me. What are we doing, I wondered, putting the future of psychotherapy into the hands of people who can't remember that the Treaty of Versailles was signed in 1871?

26

Fragment of a Medieval Auditor

Auditors are key players in the grants world. Although many people have never met one, it turns out that auditors have been around for a lot longer than any of us ever suspected.

I learned that some years ago when I was at the Bodleian Library in England, doing research on the medieval poem "Winner and Waster." While I was looking at the original manuscript of the text, I happened across a fragment of vellum slipped between the leaves. Once I examined it closely, I realized that I had stumbled across a lost fragment of the "Prologue" to Chaucer's *Canterbury Tales*.

The "Prologue," as you will recall, describes thirty or so pilgrims who made a journey to Canterbury to expiate their sins through the intercession of St. Thomas. What was in my hands was apparently a draft of a description of yet another pilgrim — an auditor — who never survived to make the pilgrimage or to be included in the final version of the *Tales*.

As nearly as I can make out, Chaucer had intended to include the auditor as company for the reeve. But there are hints that an argument broke out at the Tabard Inn, where the pilgrims had gathered to begin their journey, between Harry Bailey, its proprietor, and the auditor. The auditor had checked his tab and accused Bailey of overcharging him.

Given the hard feelings engendered so early in the trip, Chaucer seems to have thought better of including the auditor

on the pilgrimage. It is unfortunate, of course, that he was ejected
from the company because the auditor, as much as any other
pilgrim, could have used the intercession of St. Thomas to help
atone for his sins.

The lost fragment is printed here. I have modernized the
Middle English somewhat to make for easier reading. In the few
places where the text is corrupt or damaged, I have reconstructed
it, but little can be done to change the rough meter Chaucer
would surely have smoothed out had he finished the vignette.

Remember to sound the final "e" unless the following word
begins with a vowel.

> An auditor ther came, a wiley one
> From backe East to ruin alle thir fun.
> Sallow he was, as spare as is a stake
> And when he talked, he hissed lyk a snake.
> His glasses were of wyre, perched hie on his nose.
> Dressed he was in a moteley pile of clothes.
> With tye so narwe, drawn up tight lyk a noose
> He never, lyk those in Californie, hanged loose.
> A Penneyes shirt he wore, all colored plaide
> Beneath a striped sporte coat—the only one he hadde.
> He never wolde smile, and surly never daunce,
> But was wont so oft to look ascaunce
> At common ordinarye things that folkes wolde do,
> He wolde make a holy nun feel lyk a shrewe.
> He was, he saide, only ther to helpe,
> But his visit wolde make the whol campus yelpe
> With fear and trembling. Brestes wold be rente
> Lest he take backe to the governmente
> The ample fundes the faculty hadde gotte
> When off they sent that grant that was so hotte.
> He quoted rules with a nastie looke
> That made ech one feel lyk a common crooke.
> Books he bore, enough to fill ten thousand touns
> With CFR, ASPR (but no COGR) referacions,
> And when he spredeth out his regulacions alle
> The greatest room soon became too smalle.
> He wolde not taste of cake nor sip of ale

But was ever hot upon the audit traile,
Searching invoices, checkes, and receipts
To flushen out the clevrest deceits.
Lyk a hund, the scent he wolde never lose
Until he proved that thos lab supplies were booze.
All feared him, lest his slightest hunche
Wolde lead him to a disallowed lunche.
The way he wold check one cost after other
They swore this ess oh bee ne hadde no mother.
He wolde folwe columns up and down,
Grunting and snorting and making such a sound
About little thinges they hadde done wronge
They thanked God that they were not honge.
And then, he wolde—just to complete his sport—
Smile and ask to see the effort report.
"Vileynie and trecherye," he wolde shout.
"You are now ten thousand dollars out
Of funds you thought you spent so welle."
But they wolde sigh and think, "Oh, go to

And so the fragment breaks off. Unless a completed version surfaces, we will never know Chaucer's final feelings about the auditor. But this is no loss. No modern auditor would ever resemble this one anyway.

27

Patent Pending, Spending Never-ending

A few faculty members on our campus recently introduced motions to the academic senate, sent memos to the president, and sponsored resolutions before the board of trustees, calling for a more aggressive policy on patent development.

I had never held much hope for the patent business. It always seemed to me that spending money on patents was like buying an eighty-foot yacht and telling yourself it was an investment. But apparently it was time for me to entertain other thoughts about the enterprise.

I called some other universities to find out what they were up to. They reported the usual stuff: offices with technology managers and patent attorneys, and reams of memos imploring faculty to file disclosures in a timely fashion, resulting in a few licenses that produced a trickle of income.

There was one exception in the group, however. It was a comprehensive university near the Nevada-California border with a unique system for patent development.

"Tell me about it," I asked the director of research.

"Well, first of all," he said, "for years we ran our program like everyone else's, and like everyone else we had little to show for it. We made a tidy sum off a guy who invented an inhaler that produced momentary congestion so you could call in to work sick and really sound like it. Then we earned back our investment on a space-age-material toothpick that Harley Davidson optioned to promote its bikes among the yuppies. But beyond that, nothing.

"In ten years, we spent almost $780,000 on our patent office, attorney's fees, and venture capital, and made less than $160,000. We were losing eighty cents on the dollar, and I saw nothing to suggest that the situation would improve dramatically."

"Sounds about as bad as it could get," I said.

"Not really. The story gets worse. Our system stroked losers. Since we didn't force researchers to bring in their ideas, they kept all the good ones for themselves and brought only the clunkers to the patent committee. Every time the committee met it cost about $2,000, with almost no reasonable prospects of success."

"So what did you do?"

"One day I got so frustrated I went in to see our vice-president and told her our patent program stunk. 'We could do better,' I said, 'putting $2,000 on the double zero at roulette.'

"I was joking, of course, but her eyes lit up. She asked me how it would work.

" 'Well,' I said, 'It's simple. The roulette wheel pays 92 percent. Statistically, placing $2,000 on the **00** every time we think of pursuing a patent should yield four times more than our current route of patent to licensing to development to product to market to royalties.'

"She thought for a second and then told me to go for it, as long as I could hide it so no one ever found out what we were doing. I thought about zero-based budgeting and how no one ever asks about that anymore. So I figured that twice as much would be twice as unnoteworthy. I called the new approach the 'Double Zero-Based Patent Development System.'

"I was right. The term sounded like we were getting down below bedrock to work our way up. No one was ever interested in the details. That is, not until you called."

"Has it worked?" I asked.

"So far. In fact, even though our administrative premise has been kept secret, we've worked out a high-profile approach that stresses the benefits to our educational program."

"How do you manage that?"

"We use students. Our educational philosophy emphasizes

learning by doing. Whenever our committee approves a patent for exploitation, we send it to our engineering faculty with a few bucks for materials and supplies. They find some students who take the stuff to the computer-aided design lab and make blueprints. Then our seniors in industrial engineering manufacture one or two prototypes. We display these in the lobby in front of our patent office.

"To complete the scheme, we have students in the business school work out a marketing plan. The challenge to make these products look saleable turns our students on. You should see the four-color promotional brochures they put together. These kids could sell pantyhose to orangutans. I'll send you a couple."

"No thanks," I said. "I don't wear pantyhose. So how has it worked?"

"Great. In the first year the payoff was $216,000 from $266,000 invested. The best thing is, it's cheap to run. We've got plenty of volunteers to go to Las Vegas. All we do is pay their expenses.

"The low operating cost makes the numbers incredible. Administration now costs a tenth of what it used to. Without lawyers to pay, the reports look like we've finally turned our program around. We're thirteenth in the country in income, and our cost/earnings ratio ranks with the best."

"What do you do with the money left over from administration?" I asked.

"We put it into an account for special projects. The first one turned into a windfall. We spent it on this new guy in our annual giving office. He hatched a scheme for pumping up our corporate matching-gift contributions."

"How does it work?"

"Slick. The guy locates alums who are working for companies that match employee gifts three dollars to one. Then he tells them that for every hundred dollars they donate, they'll get a ticket for a drawing for an all-expenses-paid trip to Hawaii for two, worth about a thousand bucks. He also lets it slip that there will be only ten tickets per drawing, so they can see that the payout here is 100 percent—even better than the roulette wheel.

"It turns out that a lot of our better-heeled alums buy ten tickets, which guarantees them a win. A few months later they get to read their names in the annual giving report as campus benefactors while they're sucking tax-free piña coladas under the palms."

"Then how do you come out ahead?"

"We lose on the alum's gift, but don't forget the three-to-one match. For every $1,000, the company adds $3,000. These are the bucks that make the plan pay."

"How much have you made?"

"$380,000 last year alone."

"Wow! What did you do with it?"

"We put it into our patent development program."

28

Ask Ann Granters: The Sequel

DEAR ANN: Recently we've been receiving letters from societies that want us to treat our laboratory animals better. The letters lob in like mortars, accusing us of all sorts of random crimes. Some of the letters are from legitimate organizations, but others look like they're from outfits made up of a bunch of cranks. How can I tell which is which?

SHELL SHOCKED

DEAR SHELL: Most of the organizations that seek to protect animals are legitimate, but some aren't. The telltale sign is on the envelope that carries the letter. The cranks are so reactionary they still use the two-digit postal zone inserted between the city and state. That's because they compile their mailing lists from the back pages of forty-year-old collegiate dictionaries they bought at used book stores, the same places they get most of their information.

The way they target campuses for surveillance goes something like this: if a university teaches, it has a biology department; if it has a biology department, it has animals; if it has animals, it is mutilating them. So in the interest of protecting those animals, they perpetuate one of humankind's most inhumane habits—the sending out of form letters. These letters threaten demonstrations if the recipient does not cease and desist from a laundry list of offenses against animality.

Now many of these folks think animals are superior to humans because they never kill anything unless they are planning to eat it. If animals are superior, I think it's because they never send out form letters, either for pleasure or for dinner.

As for the legitimate animal protection societies, they know what your zip code is. They're well staffed from the settlement of a class-action suit against Mutual of Omaha for invasion of privacy. The animals whose lives were pried into weekly on "Wild Kingdom" never showed up to collect their share of the award, but representatives of several of the societies did. No one in court ever asked them where they got the paw prints on their proxies.

$ $ $

DEAR ANN: I'm honked. I finally got a grant so I can do my own thing, and now I have to follow all these rules. It's my money, isn't it? I mean the campus would never have seen this grant if I hadn't written the proposal. Why won't they let me spend the money like I want?

NO CHUMP FROM NODUNK U

DEAR NO: You suffer from a common belief that campus rules ought to be suspended because you now have your own money. Don't feel alone. Most faculty members think that when they get a grant, they're in business for themselves.

Unfortunately, except in the case of fellowships, you never got a grant—the institution did. That's the legal fact. So you have to conduct it within the local rules. The sponsor is counting on that happening. That's part of the reason it gave the money to the institution, not to you.

There is another relevant issue. In a study of how grants are made, peer reviewers were given proposals to read that had already been judged in an earlier review. For some proposals the campuses where the principal investigators worked were switched. Some of the successful proposals were identified with prestigious institutions; others were listed as coming from relatively unknown campuses. Interestingly, the peer reviewers more often recommended the same proposal for funding when they thought it came from an elite university than they did when they thought it came from a second-echelon institution.

The study points out that the halo effect counts in the peer review process and is further evidence that it wasn't you, but your institution, that got the grant. Though now that I think about it, since you are from an unknown campus (what is Nodunk U anyway—Podunk without basketball?), you really do seem to have gotten the grant on your own.

$ $ $

DEAR ANN: I know that your column is directed primarily toward the grant-lorn, and that the problems of a grants administrator fall outside its pale. But I am so concerned about this that I just had to write.

Sometimes I get invited to a cocktail party or a wine-and-cheese reception with the faculty. Then someone who hasn't done a thing in fifteen years spots me and decides this is a good time to sound like his head is a cask of intellectual ferment. So he takes a half hour of my time rambling on about the things he's been thinking of and ends up asking me to send him a list of possible sponsors. I was supposed to have been taking notes all the while.

Ann, please tell them that I go to cocktail parties for the same reason they do. To get smashed.

SMUSH

DEAR SMUSH: You told them better than I ever could. Thanks for sharing.

$ $ $

DEAR ANN: Our chair in the chemistry department is not very supportive of our efforts to get research funding, so we are going outside to look for a new person. We figure we need someone with a fresh perspective. What do you think?

LOOKING OUTSIDE

DEAR LOOKING: Samuel Johnson said that a second marriage is the triumph of hope over experience. The same can be true of hiring academic heads from outside. Sometimes I suspect that faculty members don't really want someone with a fresh perspective; rather, they want someone who is ignorant of local politics so they can pull the wool over his or her eyes. Usually it's been a long time since they've been able to do so with the incumbent, which is what makes them unhappy with him or her in the first place.

But the naïveté factor lasts for only a short while. Once the outsider catches on to the scams (it takes about two years to work up a reliable book), the jig is up, the faculty members get together to vote "no confidence," and the search resumes.

Good luck. Just remember, you're not buying a solution, you're only buying time.

29

Pathology at the Research Site

We all worry, some of us more than others. But happily it turns out that all of us have less reason to worry than we think we do. A recent study has shown that of all those things we worry about only one in eight turns into a problem. Thus, 87.5 percent of the time, we are putting energy out that we don't need to.

Put another way, the passing grade in life is only 12.5 percent, a lot lower than the 65 or 70 percent we're used to from our formal education. The universe is incredibly forgiving, and at this rate we are presumably getting away with hundreds of gaffs no one will ever find out about.

Since only 12.5 percent of the things we worry about happen, should we be concerned that our worrying is inefficient? Should we stop worrying altogether on the premise that if we did so the other 12.5 percent would disappear as well?

Maybe not. It's possible that worrying about that fraction of possibilities is important to the overall well-being of society, just as fires are essential to regenerate the ecological system in forests. If that's the case, one-eighth sounds fine, just about right if I were organizing a socioecological system.

Most of my daily worries come from dealing with faculty members who don't worry enough about the things I want them to worry about. That makes me dedicate some of my time to worrying for them. To find out if my worries are well spent, I regularly visit project sites. I want to see if what I visualized when I signed a proposal is what is really happening.

One of my low-level concerns is that sooner or later I'll discover something way out of line that I would have caught had I been awake when I read the proposal. When it happens, it will probably be on a project involving human subjects.

I picture something like this: A loosely worded protocol says that research will study the efficacy of focused vs. longitudinal motivation among workers on civil engineering projects. The proposal goes before the Institutional Review Board for the Use of Human Subjects.

In this worst-case scenario, the board has gone off on a tangent. Rather than discuss content, it becomes entangled in the question of whether the principal investigator should pay his research subjects. Because there are hundreds of subjects, the principal investigator plans to use students from introductory courses. The board wonders if there is a conflict of interest here. Is the P.I. oiling the epidermis of his professional reputation with the olay of his students?

The principal investigator himself doesn't help. During the committee interview his visage is as still as any of the faces on Mt. Rushmore. He scorns questions as intrusions into his academic freedom, answering in monosyllables only after leaning momentarily to the side as if to consult with imaginary counsel.

The board becomes frustrated in its attempts to pry information loose. Eventually, it concludes that cost of payment for the subjects is the operative factor. Since he proposes using the whole freshman and sophomore general education classes for the experimental group alone, he would need a separate grant just for remuneration. The proposal is approved for submission without payment to the subjects.

To set the stage for the whole scenario, you have to visualize the preceding words as if they were white letters displayed from the bottom of a wide movie screen, slanting backward to disappear into infinity, à la *Starwars*.

The project has come up for renewal. I am seated next to the principal investigator in a four-wheel drive jostling toward the study site. The conversation is desultory, as if it were a continuation of the human subjects review board meeting.

To amuse myself in the silence, I run through mental versions of car games we used to play when I was a kid. Then I think about baseball, food, music—anything to relieve the monotony.

Nothing works.

I think about the P.I.'s recalcitrance, about how it dominates the small world of the vehicle. Why, I wonder, do I let this character write the score while I hum the tune?

I remember that old country and western song—which we could probably pick up by now on any of the local AM stations—"Hit me, beat me, make me write bad checks." It's time to take control of the situation.

"You had a rather large number of subjects," I say. "What was it, about 8,000 in the experimental cohort?" I use "rather large" to cover myself in case sampling is out and megadesign is the new trend in construction management research methodology.

"Yes."

"Well, it's good to get conclusive results when you can. Nail that hypothesis home, I always say. No one will have to replicate this study when you're done, right?"

His response has one fewer syllable than the last.

I wonder if I'm not supposed to ask questions which, when answered with one word, could be construed as placing a whole paragraph in his mouth.

We left our college town behind an hour ago. We're traveling east to a construction site, motoring into a semidesert. The sun will be above the horizon soon. I fiddle with my thermos and pour another cup of coffee.

I had no time to review the interim reports before our departure. I struggle to recall details of the proposal while a deep-seated urge leads me to question the sphinx one more time.

"Any trends in the data yet?" I ask.

"Some."

The question "Just exactly what is the idea behind focused and longitudinal motivation?" is writhing in my brain, squirming like a cobra. But by now I know better than to ask. I'll find out soon enough, I tell myself.

The vehicle climbs a steep hill. I rehearse silently the many reasons to put aside my anxiety. This guy has three major research projects under way. He sits on eight national and international panels and boards. He's respected throughout the world and was recently inducted into the prestigious Select Society for the Last Analysis.

As I chastise myself for letting my paranoia do a jig beneath the brim of my safari hat, the vehicle reaches the top of a grade and lurches to a stop at the side of the road, facing directly east. The morning sun crashes down onto the windshield, flaring out over the dust-laden glass, almost obscuring the panorama beneath.

Everything is golden—desert, rocks, air.

Shading my eyes, I can discern on the valley floor the outlines of a huge trapezoidal structure. Moving toward it are two long lines of people, one stretching off to my right as far as I can see, the other straggling off to the left. At the end of each line is what appears to be a stone block the size of a garage.

I take out my binoculars. Now I can see the lines clearly, and the mysterious stone. People dressed in short smocks are scattered alongside the right line. They have stubby batons and occasionally thrust them toward the people standing in line. On the left, those standing next to the line have sticks too, but theirs have flexible strips attached to them which they work over the heads of the subjects like fly rods.

I look a bit closer and then begin to sweat. The jargon of the research protocol clicks into meaning: focused vs longitudinal motivation.

"Cattle prods vs. whips?" I ask.

"Yep."

"That trapezoid back there—that's going to be a pyramid?"

"Yep."

Phantasm complete.

Too late do I recall that among the P.I.'s distinctions was founding member of the Society for Compulsive Anachronism. It's now apparent that his experimental research project is a ruse for constructing a final resting place for his munificence.

Just as I begin to wonder how I'm going to explain this to the vice-president, the film runs out and the screen blasts a brilliant white. The scene beneath vanishes, and the moment has come when I remind myself that this was only fantasy, just a worry given shape in a horrifying daydream.

Still, once my eyes have adjusted, I make a note to send the deans a memorandum asking them to be alert to any irregularities in off-campus research project sites using human subjects.

30

Conflict? No Problem

Years ago, when conflict of interest was a simple concept, a one-line reference in an administrative manual could handle the issue. Our campus policy said you could use campus property only for official state business; using it for private gain constituted a conflict. Anyone could follow that.

Then politicians discovered the issue. Or rather it discovered them, and to draw attention away from their own infractions, the pot called the thimble black. Legislators accused universities of wide-scale conflict and used the standard federal approach to problem solving: regulatory overkill.

In regulatory overkill, the federal government fires an outlandish set of rules across the bow of the universities. This salvo sets the outer limits to absurdity on the topic by describing every conceivable infraction and requiring the campuses to set controls for them. In the case of conflict of interest, the federal regulators not only wanted the campuses to govern all faculty members for possible conflict, but they also extended control to all administrators and staff in the review chain as well.

The reason regulatory overkill appeals to the feds is that once they issue the final rules, the regulations they print in the *Federal Register* look so lame by comparison to the original ones that the campuses are supposed to act grateful instead of outraged.

But it doesn't work that way. It's the faculty members who

have to live with the regulations, and they have no idea how absurd the regulations were when they first appeared. All they know is that some campus administrator is trying to tell them to do something that seems even more idiotic than the new regulation that was announced in the last research communiqué.

So it's up to the research administrator to figure out how to sell the faculty on a new set of rules. Fortunately, campuses have gotten a big boost in communicating about new regulations by using hotlines. Our campus has used them successfully for lobbying, antikickback, and a drug-free workplace, so it was natural to put one in for conflict of interest, in anticipation of the regulations becoming final.

To staff it, we called up a platoon of seasoned lawyers from our reserves and garrisoned them temporarily in the Misconduct Hotline Center until the architects could draw up plans for a permanent unit between the Human Subjects Compliance Plaza and the Animal Welfare Maze.

So far the hotline has worked well. Through it we've helped hundreds of callers with significant, significant-but-not-con-flicted, significant-but-waived, insignificant, and so-insignificant-as-not-to-cause-an-impediment situations.

Rather than go into great detail describing the theory, it seems easiest to give examples of how the system works. Since we monitored the first several hundred calls, we have a complete record of the initial hour and a half of operation. The following excerpts are drawn from the tapes. (Freedom from Litigation Legislation prohibits the publication of what the callers said, so only the lawyers' responses are printed.)

INTEREST IN CONFLICT

a half-act play
in four parts

Hello, hello. You're on the air. Could you turn down your radio. We seem to be getting feedback.

Heh, heh, just a little joke. Of course we're not being recorded. That would be against the law. So what's your name?

I'd like one, that's why. It helps personalize the conversation.

Then give me one you've always wanted to be called.

Okay, Eunice. Now may I have your social security number?

It's for a game we play here. We've got a chart on the wall with all the social security numbers in the country. When we get a call, we cross out that number. We want to see how many we can get.

Thanks.

One more thing. Is your problem hypothetical, are you calling for a friend, or are you doing this as a class project?

Hypothetical? Great. They're a lot easier to handle than cases for friends.

You don't think this one will be?

Okay, I'll listen carefully.

[time, time]

Let me get this straight. The wife of a principal investigator is upset because her husband is wrapped up in his research career and is ignoring her. She has become involved with her husband's graduate assistant and wants a divorce. But he won't give her one because he doesn't believe in divorce except in the case of death.

What is that, some kind of cult belief?

Oh, his own death. Yeah, I've heard of that kind. Different. What does he think lawyers are for? Never mind. Go on.

She secretly moved her private fortune into investments that will profit from his research?

I see where this is going. His colleagues will get wind of it and accuse him of trying to profit unfairly from his research. That'll ruin his career and drive him to suicide, leaving her free to marry the graduate student.

Clever. How did you find out about this hypothetical case, Eunice?

From his secretary? You think she's secretly in love with the professor?

[pause]

Yes, he does seem like the unselfish sort.

No, I'd say he doesn't deserve that kind of treatment.

Yes, it does seem like his wife is victimizing an honest man with a regulation that is supposed to keep America strong, not give an uncaring tramp a way to ruin the career of someone she doesn't love anymore.

Yes, I do think something ought to be done about it.

Uh huh.

Well, we can't do that. Whatever we do, it's got to be within the law.

Please don't feel that way. Your call hasn't been wasted. We'll do something. Just lemme think.

[time]

Tell me about those investments again.

If what you say is true, you're describing a classic conflict situation. A classic. [rustle] Now where's my response checklist? Ah hah!

Okay, now listen closely. A law has been violated. We can act—indeed, we must act.

We'll send someone down right away to seal his laboratory, impound his data, and bar him from the campus until he produces convincing evidence that the conflict is not significant.

[pause]

Why are you so upset?

That's not true. You don't know that that's true about all lawyers.

That's ridiculous.

Look, we seem to be getting some static on the line. I've got to go. So thank you for calling and have a nice day.

$ $ $

Hello, hello, you're on the air.

I'm sorry, you'll have to speak more slowly. Your accent is a little heavy.

Thank you. Now what would you like?

Yes, that's a problem all right, but it's a question about scientific misconduct. We don't do misconduct here. That's another hotline.

You shouldn't be getting a busy signal. Since the whistle-blower amendment went through there are seventeen people down there, around the clock.

Well okay, maybe I can help you if it's an easy one. I got my start in misconduct.

[time]

Let's see if I have this correctly. A member of your department has published an article with bad data, and you believe he did so on purpose.

You're the department chair and you want to handle it before it comes to a misconduct hearing. Wonderful!

Huh?

No, we don't pay attention to which hand collected the spurious data. Why?

Well actually, we don't follow that practice in our society. We consider it ghoulish.

Because we figure once they get out of prison, they will need both to work with, that's why. Two come in handy. For manual labor. From the Latin *manus*, meaning "hand."

I know where you come from they handle these cases differently. But we are a country of law, not of retribution. Generally, we think going to court is punishment enough.

Oops, I've got another call. Look, why don't you keep trying the misconduct lines. I'm sure that once you get through they can help you better than I can.

Bye.

$ $ $

Hello, hello. You're on the air.

Yes, I realize the regulations say you can't use state facilities for private purposes.

No, that doesn't mean you have to go across the street to the gas station.

[pause]

It is perfectly legitimate for you to go down the hall and use the facilities there.

[big pause]

I know the rules say you can only use state facilities for official business, but you're taking them too literally.

Look, everyone else is doing it, aren't they? Do they look guilty?

I know that a rule is a rule, but you gotta lighten up about this.

All right, then try this: why not pretend that while you're down there, you're actually doing official state business.

It's not absurd at all. Sometimes when I leave here to go down the hall, what I'm doing down there seems an awful lot like what I'm doing when I'm up here.

Now you're pushing it. No way could you draw overtime for doing it in your off hours.

Wait a second, I've got a call on another line and I'm the only one here.

No, that's lobby noise, not other lawyers. I'm working here alone until I can get my own office.

I haven't got time to argue. I'll get back to you in a few minutes.

Bye.

$ $ $

Hello, hello. You're on the air.

No, the regulations don't cover animals used in the research. How could an animal have a conflict?

[time]

Let me make sure I've got this right. You were doing behavioral research with porpoises on nonverbal communication, and the results show that the human brain can act like a receiver and pick up radio waves? Now people won't need cellular telephones. They can buy pills from the company that sponsored the research and stimulate the data receptors in their brains.

How long does the effect last?

About three minutes. That's cute. So how do you dial?

Well as time goes on you may want to develop a more sightly way than working your tongue like you're picking popcorn hulls out of your teeth. Now what's your problem?

The paper describing the results is due out tomorrow. Uh huh. And you just found out that a retired Sea World porpoise used in the experiment has an IRA that is heavily invested in the company that holds the patent on the chemical compound.

Sea World has a retirement program for its animals?

Oh, just for the performing ones.

So now you think the porpoise was faking its responses and all the data you got from it was actually testimony.

But porpoises can't fake chemical reactions.

I know we once thought they couldn't communicate either, but controlling their own chemical reactions??

Okay, I suppose that even if we know it can't happen, the public may believe it can. So what?

I see. The stock. It may take off, and then drop like a rock once the news about the porpoise gets out.

So you think the porpoise ought to divest?

Now let's get serious for just a minute. How could the porpoise ever have found out about the stock market in the first place?

You think it's been picking up "Moneyline" from communications satellites and tracking E.T. Ltd.?

What's that, an over-the-counter stock?

[pause]

When does the announcement hit the *Times?*

Um, excuse me, I've got a call on another line. Could I put you on hold for just a minute?

[dial, dial]

Hello, Charlie? Listen, I don't have much time to talk right now because I'm on another line.

Yeah, two lines going all the time, just like you guys.

Look, here's the deal. I want you to sell all my mutual funds and buy an over-the-counter-stock called E.T., hold it for five days, and then dump it.

I don't care if you never heard of the company before. Neither had I until just a few minutes ago. But I've got a hunch.

No, I can't tell you where I got the hunch.

Believe me, I can't.

That would be a conflict of interest.

31

Animal Welfare Protection: How Much Is That Doggie in the Window?

I got a call from Washington, D.C., the other day. The person on the line wanted to know when we were going to bring our animal use policies into line with the Health Research Act of 1985.

I had tried to comply with the new rules when the draft regulations first came out but had gotten into trouble fast. The regs were vague and/or (to use their phraseology) contradictory. I didn't know how to handle the requirement for equitable treatment and recognition, so I went to the memorandum of understanding with our faculty union for some ideas and lifted some of its wording about how to evaluate workload.

That's what got me into trouble. I proposed that for each laboratory animal we log the number of projects, hours in experimental versus control groups, and number of publications resulting from the trials. I threw in a ranking system to ensure that every animal got a decent shake before retirement.

Our academic senators recoiled. They seized on the wording out of context and charged that some of the animals, favored in promotion because of their species, would advance through the ranks more quickly than the faculty. The problem stemmed from wording that was interpreted to guarantee animals coauthorship on publications. The faculty argued that even though the articles were published in prestigious journals, none of these animals had degrees from accredited institutions and were therefore in-eligible for advancement beyond the equivalent rank of lecturer.

The animal advocates countered that implicit in affirmative animal action policies was the sense that normal qualifications could sometimes be bent in the interest of equity. Besides, they argued, most publications list every research assistant who ever wandered through the laboratory anyway, so why not the animals? Indeed, the fancy footwork of many of the animals through the mazes had turned many a weak research protocol into a publishable product.

To solve the impasse, the university appointed a blue-ribbon group called "The 2001 Committee"—referring to the expected date of the final report—to study the issues. The call from Washington, then, was a blessing. I needed help now.

"What's up?" I asked the caller.

She said she wanted to know how the broadened representation on the animal welfare committee was coming: did we have a nonscientist, a nonuniversity person, a non- . . . ?

"Hold on," I interrupted. "I know you want to make sure that our research animals receive humane treatment, but let me tell you something: these regulations offer a lot more guidance than we would ever need. We have a very small animal research program.

"In fact," I quipped, "we have so few animals that when we hold our committee meetings, all the animals attend, and they even get to vote."

Colleagues have told me that my fatal flaw is not being able to resist a quip even when I'm dead certain it will get me into trouble. This was one of those times. My internal chortle had only just begun when it hit me that she might take the comment seriously.

She did. She said she was glad we were so egalitarian. She said she would note that when she wrote up her report.

"When's your next meeting?" she asked.

"Thursday afternoon."

"I'll be there," she said. "I want to see this. Please have all the members present."

"All?" I asked.

"All," she said firmly.

I was in trouble. Site visits are intended solely to determine if reality checks out with our preposterous claims about it. They're worse than a blind date.

We had two days to get ready. I decided that the easiest way to handle the situation was to dress up some graduate students in last spring's Mardi Gras costumes. That gave us a bear in a tutu, a chimp in a locomotive engineer's outfit, a rabbit in a tuxedo, and a two-part horse for which seating would be problematic.

We set a dry run for Thursday morning before our guest's visit. It went dismally. The graduate students, arriving in animal drag, would not reveal who was who. They goofed off and quipped relentlessly. The bear said she thought professors were soul mates because they were always hibernating in their laboratories. The rabbit nattered on about how hard it was having his reputation for sexual prowess eclipsed by some of the professors. The chimp squirted oil in the joints of all the table, chairs, and committee members.

Threats to withhold grades were of no avail. Promises of extra credit failed. Without the normal means of controlling their every move, the faculty had no power over the students.

I signaled the veterinarian, who herded the students into a corner, tranquilized them with a dart gun, and immediately shipped them to the wild.

Time was running out. The real animals, I thought, could be no worse a behavior problem. After all, we had been treating them like humans for a long time. The veterinarian went down to the vivarium to get them.

They filed into the conference room, some with copies of *Born Free* stuck under their arms, just as our visitor from the National Institutes of Health (NIH) arrived.

The meeting began with the chair introducing the first research protocol for review: a gall bladder transplant. No sooner was the project on the table than a marmoset interrupted.

"First of all," she said, "I would like to thank our visitor from the NIH for the recent ruling that allows us to receive mail. Second, I want to thank Penny Patterson of the Gorilla Foundation, the woman who taught Koko to speak, for the marvelous correspondence course she put together in animal speech.

"And third," she said, turning toward the chair, "before you go any further with review of this protocol, I want to know where the results of the invertebrate trials are."

"Huh?"

"The invertebrate trials," she repeated. "You know, beetles and bugs. The regulations are clear. No researcher may try a procedure on a mammal until it has been thoroughly tested on insects. The only exception is a documented emergency. If you have a writ, you can skip the trials and go directly to mammals."

The veterinarian was flipping furiously through the guidelines hidden between his knees to find the stuff about invertebrate trials. He was also beginning to wish he were a vegetarian, though he wasn't sure why. Then he heard a giggle.

"Just kidding," the marmoset chattered. "I wanted to see if you would take us seriously. Bugs don't have gall bladders."

The chair was opening his mouth to say he knew that all along when a guinea pig interrupted.

"Well, you might be joking, but I'm not about to blow this chance to make a statement. I've used all the passes allowed me to go down to the regulations library and study the rules. You know what the rules say about exposing us to unwarranted stress?" He leaned closer to the microphone. His whiskers grated against the windscreen. The sound of his heavy voice filled the room. "Nowhere but nowhere do any of those regs even hint that you can do what you're doing to us. Making us attend a committee meeting clearly falls in the category of cruel and unusual treatment."

Then he broke down in laughter.

"Yeah," yucked a baboon. "We'll report you to the Animal Welfare Committee."

"Enough of the comedy," scowled a rat. "You guys are wasting a valuable opportunity. I want to talk about serious stuff, like letting us rats live together. Visiting privileges aren't enough. You spend a few months in those cages without the usual needs of life being met and strange things start to happen.

"Why just last week my brain started flashing stuff that don't make sense, like eek equals em see with a little high two. I don't need junk like that rattlin' around in my head. What I need is some regular sex."

A linguistics expert was there to help us interpret the animals' comments. I looked at his notepad. It was covered with scratch marks, swirls, and squiggles. They looked like the consent signatures we gather from the animals before we can allow them to participate in a research project.

"Did you send around a sign-in sheet before I got here?" I asked.

"That's my phonetic transcription," he hissed.

"Oh," I said. I turned my attention back to the table.

"That's an interesting point about sex," the chair said, "but the regulations tell us the most important thing for you is clean cages and fresh water daily. Don't you want that?"

"Hey," said the rat, his voice raspy. "I don't think much about fresh water and clean cedar shavings when I'm pasted up against the wire panting at Ratsetta over there. That's one dynamite rat."

He motioned toward the prettiest black rat you've ever seen. She was sitting demurely on a chair against the wall. Her white mascara was streaking. Until then she hadn't been sure of his feelings.

"We'll see what we can do," the chair said, trying to skirt the issue. "Any other points before we get on with the agenda?"

"Yeah, I've got a beef," a monkey said.

"Boo, hiss," went the animals.

"Sorry about that," he corrected. "I mean 'a complaint.' I'm tired of faking the human act, exaggerating the human side of me to get a decent meal."

"Yeah," piped up another. "You don't know what it's like, listening to you guys talk in the lab about us, like the only reason you keep us around at all is our human qualities. In fact, all this has messed up my own sense of self. When I came here I was looking forward to learning more about what it was to be a monkey. Now I find I want to please you more than I want to be me. I just keep giving and giving. But—" there was a catch in his voice, "—I'm losing my sense of monkeyness. I don't know who I . . ."

The creature began to sob.

The chair tried to explain.

"Look, we don't have any choice about how to treat you.

It's all set by law. The government tells us to look out for your comfort and basic needs for food and cleanliness. We figured the rest would take care of itself. We had no idea about this other stuff."

"But we're all individuals," said a scruffy rat. "We should be treated as such. Look, I ain't trying to kid nobody. I been a bum all my life and ain't never had nuttin' so nice as that stainless-steel rectangular cage.

"But Edith over there, she's a city rat. She's used to high rises, elevators, a hole with a view. When she was just a mouse she left the country to take her chances in the city, to find her fortune and a hot pastrami sandwich at two in the morning. She succeeded. That is, until she got picked up for loitering and was brought here. Now look at what she's got."

"Speaking of hot pastrami," said another, "let's talk about the menu we get before we are, as you so mincingly put it, 'sacrificed.' We were thinking maybe a little gravy sloshed over the dry food would be appropriate. Do you guys have a recipe for a pellet bisque?"

That's the way it went. I began to think we should have stuck with the grad students. But it was too late now. I worked to maintain the pretense that this was daily fare.

Our visitor never spoke a word until the meeting was adjourned. Then she said she'd seen what she needed and left on the next flight.

We never got a report. We learned later that upon her return she resigned her job at the NIH and resumed her former position at the Department of Defense, where she had designed recreation programs for enlisted men.

As for the graduate students, we still get postcards from them expressing their gratitude.

32

Take It to the Public

For years, workshops about grant writing touted the rifle approach. "Target your sponsor," they'd say. And so thousands of grant hopefuls followed suit, carefully aiming each proposal at a specific sponsor. It was tedious, time-consuming, hard work.

Then some of them discovered that having lunch with a senator was a lot easier than writing a full-length proposal. The experience showed that a laboratory or a center could be funded without the tedium of composing a 150-page text. A gift of a bottle of Napoleon brandy from the governor, a cocktail party with a slight touch of class, and *wahlah* (as today's high school sophisticates say in their best hallway French), a new research laboratory is born. The approach broke the stranglehold of writing individual proposals.

Still, some scientists can't stand the thought of cozying up to a senator with bad breath just to get a new lab. They believe they deserve research funds for no reason other than that it's a good idea to have them, like pink flamingos on the front lawn. To them, research funding ought to come as easily as going down the hall to get chemical supplies.

If this is ever going to happen, they will need to cut out the middlemen and take their story directly to their constituency, to skip the bureaucrats and Congress and go right to the American people. After all, as anyone who ever wrote a commercial will tell you, it's the people who have the money.

In the world of communications this means it's time for the research world to use the mass media.

Why not? Where would Henry Ford's heirs be today if every time someone wanted a car Henry sent his designers to the drafting board for a fresh idea? Just as the Model T became the muumuu of the auto industry, so we should be able to concoct a one-size-fits-all approach to funding research. And still have time for golf.

Some institutions are already getting into the act. Consortia of universities are beginning to lobby the public directly for support. One group, located on the West Coast, is using its proximity to Hollywood to good advantage. Called the National Organization for 'Ncouraging Extravagance toward Research and Development for Society (NONERDS), the association seeks to promote greater public awareness about research through public service announcements.

One example looks at geographical patterns in research funding. It follows the "amazing facts" formula, the one that goes:

> "Did you know that 53 percent of all automobile ac-
> cidents happen within two miles of home? And that 29
> percent happen within one block? And that 12 percent come
> to rest within inches of the trash can at the end of the
> driveway?
>
> "Drive if you must, but please, park your car two miles
> from home and take a cab.
>
> "This public service message brought to you by
> GDPMA, your Greater Downtown People Movers Author-
> ity."

NONERDS's script goes something like this:

> [The TV camera dollies in on a tanned researcher dressed
> in an oversized Hawaiian shirt. Palm trees and an ocean
> beach are visible in the background. The researcher looks
> up intently from the surfboard he has been waxing.]
>
> "Did you know," he questions, "that 40 percent of all

research grants made by the federal government are awarded within a 300-mile radius of Washington, D.C., and that half of that area is water?

"Did you know that there are 2,847 institutions of higher learning in America and that one of them, located only sixty miles from our nation's capital, receives more research funding each year than 2,700 of these combined?

"Did you know that a prominent think tank has once again suppressed results from its studies of cognition? And that its most recent study corroborates what was hinted at in earlier reports: that no more than 16.2 percent of the gross national output of what the National Bureau of Standards defines as 'thinking' actually takes place within that 300-mile zone?"

[He swallows sincerely, like the host on "Masterpiece Theatre," and continues.]

"Actually, it's not surprising that research grants are concentrated in such a small region. The same study shows that the majority of Americans believe that thinking and suffering are synonymous, that if you're going to be productive, you have to live where the traffic is miserable, people are ornery, and the weather sucks.

"But NONERDS questions this assumption.

"Take a trip beyond the Beltway. See what this country has to offer."

[He stands up and leans his surfboard against a palm tree.]

"There's more to the rest of this country than surfing."

[The camera dollies in tight for a closeup as he squares off intently at the viewer.]

"That is," he smiles slightly, "after you've burned out on surfing."

The first run of this public service announcement campaign

is expected to follow the premier showing of a new evening soap opera based on Washington politics and bureaucracy. Modeled after "Dallas," the new series will be called "Dulles." Pundits predict that bureaucrats will have it penciled in on their desk calendars long after the series has been canceled.

To expand understanding and sympathy for the researcher's lot, NONERDS is also using inexpensive magazine ads. One approach is called "Adopt-a-Researcher." The ad features a high-contrast, black-and-white photo of a gaunt faculty member in a dilapidated laboratory. He is holding a microscope. His eyes stare out hauntingly over a caption that reads:

> HE USED TO BE PRODUCTIVE
> NOW, HE'S SIMPLY DEDUCTIVE

Below, the text runs:

> Adopt a researcher and make it possible for Professor Bahtemdaubdt to use the inductive method again.
>
> Eight years ago he stripped the rack and pinion on his Edmund Scientific microscope. With no money to repair it, he has had to use old data or write his research papers from a single focus. Lately his proposals have been rejected because his peers say they lack depth.
>
> Your tax-deductible check for $100 a month can help give Bahtemdaubdt the gift of sight through a scanning electron microscope.
>
> As a valued patron, you will receive letters monthly from your researcher in which he describes his thrill as he rebuilds his interrupted relationship with the microbe.
>
> Just clip out and return the coupon along with your bank account number. We'll do the rest.
>
> Remember, only you can break the debilitating cycle of secondary data analysis.

For business trade journals, NONERDS tried a more direct approach: "Hey, Mr. Industry Leader, write off a researcher today. For the cost of a three-martini lunch, you can protect your bottom line."

NONERDS knew the ad was bold, but when dozens of irate people called, livid with accusations of insolence, the executive director was nonplussed. The mystery continued for several days until a clerk caught a mistake that had been missed when the blueline was checked. The printer had left out the final word, so that in thirty-seven different trade magazines the ad ended: "For the cost of a three-martini lunch, you can protect your bottom."

33

A Watched Pot

For years the Department of Defense kept itself busy and rich devising ingenious ways to deliver nuclear warheads. But when the U.S. government and the Russians began to rid themselves of their nuclear arsenals and the peace dividend was being cashed in, the life-style at the DOD was put in jeopardy. The department realized it needed to find something else to worry about and to spend money on, or risk becoming just another federal bureaucracy.

One fertile possibility was to fret about whether the Russians might be plotting to destroy us in a more devious, less-verifiable way—by using parapsychological means, for example. The Pentagon was aware that the USSR had been studying psychic phenomena since World War II. But the DOD had been loathe to do its own studies of mind-over-matter phenomena. Its motto—"Go for the Gold"—had backfired and led to a trophy room full of Golden Fleece Awards. Doing studies of the parapsychological, it reasoned, could only add to the clutter of awards.

But the threat of a deep budget reduction soon outweighed the fear of getting back on Senator Proxmire's list. The brass started writing concerned memos. All indications, they said, showed that the Russians were ahead in the charms race. Reports from the '60s, which told of Russians who could make pens roll just by looking at them, were being replaced by more recent intelligence information indicating that some Russian psychics could heat objects with their gaze. Melting, the DOD reasoned, could be next.

Here was something to worry about. The generals who remembered the movie *The Day the Earth Stood Still* wrote that the time might come when they would be frantically searching through their ranks to find someone who could recall the phrase *"Katu barada niktu"* to stop the robot with the heat ray.

The DOD issued a Request for Proposal to study the state of the knowledge about the relationship between psychokinesis and heat transfer. The RFP called for a literature search and a baseline study to see whether the mind alone could affect the temperature of an inanimate object.

The Ch'n Ch'minie Institute off the Massachusetts coast won the contract. Its proposal was creative and cheap. It repeated an earlier approach it had used when Ch'n Ch'minie investigators tested hundreds of medieval herbal remedies for the National Institutes of Health to see if any would cure modern ailments. With this single approach the institute had delivered lots of good medicine to the NIH inexpensively. All the NIH had to do was give Latin names to wortplant and snoutgrass so that such could be prescribed through modern pharmacies.

The project had doubled the NIH's clout on Capitol Hill. The same process, Ch'n Ch'minie reasoned, could work for the Department of Defense. The institute proposed to study traditional sayings to see what could be learned from the past. It decided to review proverbs about mind over matter. "A watched pot never boils" was selected as the most promising. If the Russians were onto something, Ch'n Ch'minie figured, it would find a clue here.

Common sense says that a pot should boil more quickly when someone is watching it. And common sense seemed to be consistent with the direction Russian research was taking. But if the counterintuitive indication of the watched pot proverb was right, then the opposite would happen. That is, people in their natural state would slow down rather than speed up the heating process. Then the DOD would know that the reports from Russia were phoney and that this branch of psychic phenomenon was worthless.

The watched pot hypothesis was elegant because it could

test two major scientific principles at once: the Heisenberg Principle in physical science and the Hawthorne Effect in social science. The Heisenberg Principle says that if you watch something closely, just watching it will make it do something else. This phenomenon is most easily observable at the level of subatomic particles. But we see it work at the macrolevel as well. For instance, if you watch the stock market closely enough, it *will* go down. Contrariwise, if you watch kids closely, nothing will happen, but as soon as you stop, all hell will break loose.

Running completely counter to the Heisenberg Principle is the Hawthorne Effect. It says that if you watch something, it will do the same thing it's been doing, only better — what everyone hoped for when they started watching the pot in the first place. The effect was first noticed in a study of productivity at AT&T's Hawthorne Works in Cicero, Illinois. Workers were told that they were being watched to see if changes made in working conditions would increase productivity.

Then the researchers introduced conditions and practices known to decrease productivity. They dimmed the lights and painted the walls unpleasant colors. Despite these counterproductive steps, the workers worked harder. The researchers concluded that the workers worked harder simply because they were grateful for the attention and wanted to please. We expect no less of a watched pot.

With this two-pronged approach, one of the researchers reviewed the literature and reported to the group that it was skewed and had missed some obvious questions. He noted, for instance, that all the Russian studies assumed it was the subject who had the power to make the pen roll. No one ever checked to see whether the pen had any say in the matter. Maybe, he suggested, some pens moved because they became self-conscious about being stared at.

"Let's say that, much earlier in their evolution, pens moved a lot, sometimes because they themselves wanted to and other times because someone else wanted them to. Then they got some good therapists — penologists, I suppose — who helped them stop rolling to the bidding of others. Some of the pens may just not have completely internalized that freedom yet.

"Imagine a pen on a couch. The therapist is saying, 'You

don't have to roll just because someone else wants you to. Ask yourself what is it that *you* want to do. There's nothing more self-demeaning than being on a roll that's not your own.' "

When the researcher finished postulating his theory, the rest of the team exchanged glances, waited until he took a break, and then replaced him on the study.

The new member ran a literature search in English-language journals to balance the reports from the Russian journals. The results were slim. One movie critic had done some penetrating work on the effects of the cold stare in the films of Clint Eastwood. Other than that, not much was found.

The team returned to the matter of devising a protocol that would control for the Heisenberg Principle and the Hawthorne Effect. It developed a multifaceted methodology to see if the eye would turn heat waves back upon themselves. Watching was to be done in single, double, and random sets. A blind wasn't enough, so a double-blind study was conducted on a second set of pots.

An array of pots was instrumented and observed through a two-way mirror so that some pots would not know the researchers were watching both while the experimental subjects watched the pots. Some team members argued that it would be better to separate the pot completely from the side effect of researcher observation by utilizing an auditory signal (a water kettle whistle). Others argued that back pressure from the lid would neutralize the effect of eye power. Then some claimed that the lid should make no difference since the saying specified a watched *pot*, not watched water *in* the pot (nine days old).

The dilemma was solved when another researcher who had been paying attention in tenth-grade English recalled that "pot" was a figure of speech called synecdoche. As used, "pot" includes the water inside, just as "keel" stands for the whole ship and "snarl" stands for the whole subway token collector. That is, she argued, if it weren't for synecdoche, a watched pot wouldn't boil because it wouldn't have any water in it. It might melt, but it would never boil, and the institute wouldn't have a pot to propose in.

All the trials were run, with consistently negative results.

To make sure, Ch'n Ch'minie tried a set of experiments

using group pressure. Twelve people were arrayed in the classic mystical diadem to ponder, stare, and gaze. Every configuration produced the same negative results. No matter what the institute tried, the parapsychological notwithstanding, a watched pot boiled in the same amount of time as an unwatched pot.

The DOD learned that it had nothing to learn except that the old saying needed to be revised. As a courtesy, the institute sent the editors of *Bartlett's Familiar Quotations* a list of substitute sayings, to wit:

> Sixty-two watched pots boiled as quickly as fifty-nine un-watched pots, whereas twenty-seven boiled nearly as quickly and thirty-two boiled slightly less quickly.

> Watching a pot until it boils does not promote the heating process but does give one a sense of involvement in an overautomated society.

> A watched pot never boils, but the water inside does.

To keep the Russians spinning their wheels, the Department of Defense published a bogus article that reported promising results. When the DOD set about to disband the parapsychological division, however, it discovered another principle it couldn't as easily rewrite: you can create ten bureaucracies more easily than you can dissolve one. Bureaucracy and entropy, it appears, are equal forces eating away at the universe from opposite edges.

34

Ann Granters Helps the Contract Administrator

DEAR ANN: There seems to be an inverse correlation at work these days. The less money involved in an agreement, the longer it takes to negotiate it. Is there a Murphy's Law I don't know about?

CONFUSED

DEAR CONFUSED: Actually, it's a Parkinsonian law. C. Northcote Parkinson named it the Law of Triviality. Briefly stated, the time spent on any item will be in inverse proportion to the amount of money involved.

Parkinson first noted the operation of the law in the early '50s in Singapore. He found that a committee will spend little time on important and complex issues but an inordinate amount of time on trivial issues. In his book, he described how the law would operate at a meeting of a hypothetical finance committee.

Say that one of the first items on the agenda is approval for the construction of a $10-million atomic reactor (in 1957 dollars). The committee has only one person knowledgeable about reactors, and just a few others with any familiarity at all with the issue. The knowledgeable person will be reluctant to monopolize discussion and so the staff report, which recommends proceeding with the contract, will be passed without comment. The process takes 2.4 minutes (in 1957 time).

Two items down, the need for a storage shed will come up.

Since many board members know something about sheds, they will question composition of material, ease of construction, length of life, and so on, before approving construction. Total time for discussion, thirteen minutes.

At the end of the agenda is the issue of continuing to provide free coffee at the monthly meeting. By now, any member feeling sheepish about not having contributed to the reactor debate or the shed question will feel constrained to inquire energetically into the appropriateness of the group's spending four point three one dollars of the body politic's money each month on its own indulgence. Vigorous debate will follow, consuming the final hour and thirty-three minutes of the meeting.

Parkinson's Law of Triviality, as you suggest, has a corollary in the grants world. Had he written about contract administration, Parkinson might have observed that the less money involved in an agreement, the longer it takes to negotiate it.

For instance, if a $16-million three-year grant is at stake, everyone will assume that any organization competent enough to have written a fundable proposal for such an amount will be competent enough to administer it. The instrument of choice will be as simple as a purchase order.

But if a local county unit is about to award $1,300 for undergraduates to run a survey, the contracting officer will float a thirty-five-page document that contains every clause he or she has ever seen designed to protect the public from fraud, sloth, malfeasance, and social and environmental irresponsibility.

Months will pass before the award is made. It will be finalized three weeks after the undergraduates have presented their conclusions, and well past the point where their behavior could have been altered to comply with any of the contract clauses in dispute.

The tendency of human nature to excel in the trivial has received a major assist recently from modern technology, which may have contributed to your raising your question in the first place.

A small firm in Boston has developed computer software that automatically writes contracts. The program scans a proposal for key words, identifies the risks associated with them, searches a data base for legal boilerplate, and then prints out a contract with all the clauses needed to manage these risks.

The software is marketed to help smaller governmental units like villages that have no lawyers on retainer. It can raise questions at the rate of forty-seven nits per mip. With it, any grantor can act like it has a legal firm on retainer with a title running into five surnames. All the village needs is $29.95 for the software.

The program pushes Parkinson's Law to the limits of mega-triviality. It is the contract administrator's nightmarish equivalent to third-world countries acquiring nuclear capability.

The main difficulty with the software is that it inserts clauses into a contract without indicating the reason for their inclusion. Thus, if it scans a proposal that has misspelled the word "un-clear" as "nuclear," the program will trigger fifty or so clauses appropriate to awards involving radiation hazards. Sifting them out is like trying to reconstitute a bowl of Grapenuts after it's been spilled on the beach.

So what do you do? Unless you have a legal firm on retainer running into *six* surnames, your best bet is to buy software from the same firm, NITMIP Softworks. It sells a program that diagnoses its own contracts and proposes alternate language.

At a suggested list price of $2,995.95, the software is a bargain.

$ $ $

DEAR ANN: We have a new president who has an open-door policy. Faculty members with innovative ideas are encouraged to come in and discuss them with her.

Generally the results have been positive. But every now and then someone walks in, reaches inside his wide-lapeled plaid sports coat, and pulls out a truly harebrained scheme.

Naturally, the president doesn't want to spend general fund dollars on wacky ideas, so she tries to ease the blow by sending the character down to me to see if we can get him a grant.

Any ideas for handling this situation without wasting a lot of time or honking off my new boss?

LAYING LOW

DEAR LYING: A Chinese economics journal, having received a proposed article of similar quality, handled the situation this way:

> We have read your manuscript with boundless delight. If we were to publish your paper, it would be impossible for us to publish any work of lower standard. And as it is unthinkable that in the next thousand years we shall see its equal, we are, to our regret, compelled to return your divine composition and to beg you a thousand times to overlook our short sight and timidity.

You can do the same kind of thing. When this character begins his spiel, listen intently. Do not move for five minutes. Then look as if you were going to take a note, stop, widen your eyes and say:

> "Stop right there. This is not simply a brilliant idea, it is a once-in-a-century concept. It is the beginning of a new millennium of thinking in your discipline. You're speaking a language that the feds won't have learned the grammar of for another hundred years.
> "But no mere bureaucrat could ever appreciate its far-reaching implications. He or she would treat it like cold fusion. We must protect against that."

Next, tell him that only another *person* of great insight and sensitivity could appreciate the elegance of this idea. Someone out on the edge, just like himself.

Then give him directions to the Development Office.

$ $ $

DEAR ANN: Every day it seems that I get a new certification to sign: antilobbying, drug-free workplace, debarment and suspension, antikickback. But I've never known anyone involved in these things. Is life passing me by?

OUT-OF-TOUCH IN ROCHESTER

DEAR ROCH: You and lots others. Hundreds of research administrators have written procedures to implement federal regulations and found no one to use them on.

Don't worry. Washington has found a way to solve that problem. The Council on Governmental Relations has just received a bootleg copy of proposed regulations called "Quota on Enforcement."

Apparently, the folks in Washington have become concerned that research administrators are setting up procedures to control for problems and then doing nothing with them. Rather than assume it's because most people on university campuses are honest, they figure it's because grants officers are gold-bricking.

So "Quota on Enforcement" ("Q on E," as we refer to it) was drafted. It's aimed at the folks the guidelines refer to as the "regulatory reluctant." Under these rules, they can be cited for lack of aggressive action.

"Q on E" builds on basic police force practices. Just as police officers are expected to write a certain number of traffic tickets, so the feds are setting minimums according to campus size and location for the number of drug users you should have busted, the number of lobbyists you should have silenced, and the number of kickbacks you should have intercepted.

The pressure to do something is going to build fast, so you had better prepare yourself for action. Here are a few things you can do now.

First, you can write to the General Services Administration for a Joe McCarthy Investigator's Kit, which comes with a one-paragraph instruction leaflet and a briefcase with a solid foam core. After all these years it still represents state of the art for investigating threats to the American fiber, and its attractive closeout price has been unaffected by thirty-five years of inflation.

Second, you can follow the lead of a few proactive universities. To meet their quota, their grants administration offices are setting up internship agreements with state and federal prisons. They will place parolees as supplementary staff in critical offices like purchasing and contracts administration.

The campuses are particularly interested in finding former CEO's from the savings and loan industry who are already coming out on parole. These people look good in the office and almost guarantee multiple infractions with a single phone call. Thus you add to quota for several different regulations at the same time.

If you want to do the same thing, you better act fast; the real losers are sure to be snapped up quickly. Get on the phone to your local penitentiary and soon you will no longer feel out of it in Rochester.

$ $ $

DEAR ANN: Every once in a while a faculty member comes in with a proposal and takes up my time with all sorts of special conditions and arrangements—last-minute letters of support, special consortial arrangements, payment for human subjects who don't have a green card, weird stuff like that.

Well, I do it, and without complaint—break my back to get the proposal out the door. Then before you can say A-21, he's arguing for a reduction in indirect costs because he doesn't see that we do anything for his money.

How come this happens? Am I

JUST A CHUMP?

DEAR JUST: Yes. You're making your job look too easy.

Lots of grants development people make the same mistake. They hang out a shingle that says nonchalantly "Grants 'n Things" and act like they can take care of the toughest problem while they're on hold on the telephone.

But making proposal review look easy only gives people the idea that you aren't working for your money. And your clients feel they've been had.

So stop it. Instead, be proactive. By that I mean get in this guy's way. Drag out some impossible regulations that were never implemented, like the conflict of interest ones, and tell him you will have to hold up his proposal while you check out the investment portfolio of his bank to make sure it doesn't have any biotechnology stock that might profit from his research and push his interest-bearing checking account up from 5.25 to 5.5 percent.

Better yet, take the thing out of the room mumbling something about misconduct, or lobbying, or whatever, and say you need to take it to legal counsel, the way the car salesman makes you cool your heels when you're trying to argue him down by saying he's got to take your offer to his manager to be okayed and you wait for a half hour while the two of them slip across the street for a margarita.

So take your sweet time. Have a daiquiri, while you're at it, for me.

If you put pain back into the process, the faculty will begin to appreciate your efforts again. They've got to believe it's a tough job before they'll give up without a fight.

$ $ $

CONFIDENTIAL TO "SITTING WITH MY BACK TO THE WALL": It sounds like you have a public relations problem. Stop stamping "As Is" on the cover sheets of proposals that come in without enough time for review. You can probably take down the "No Tipping" sign as well. And the next time you get a package without a return address, for Pete's sake open it under water.

Look for ways to help. Bend over backwards. Put out a sign that says "Grants 'n Things." Call J. A. Chump for more advice.

Ann is ready to answer your letters, too. Just send your question, a phony name, proof of grant, and a SASE to: Ask Ann Granters, P.O. Box 1326, San Luis Obispo, CA 93406.

Questions are handled in complete confidence. Federal regulations require that copies of all -lorn correspondence be retained for seven years.

Member, FDIC.

35

A Glossary of Scholarly Phraseology

Each major academic discipline has its own lexicon that explains the meaning of the words its practitioners use. Thanks to this resource, parsing a parsec takes no longer than a nanosec. Scientific, artistic, and humanistic *term*inology, then, is no mystery to the individual discipline.

But there is also a scholarly *phrase*ology that is common to all academic areas. Although there is no dictionary of usage, the best researchers know what each phrase means. Precise usage is essential to the survival of every academic scholar.

By scholarly phraseology I am referring to the webbing of words that introduces a topic and leads the reader from one idea to the next. Deftly used, this language can suspend the fruit cocktail of fragmented data long enough in the jello of uncertainty for the reader to gain the impression that he or she has glimpsed something comprehensible without being certain of what it was, but ever thereafter sure that any misapprehension owes more to the dimness of self-perception than to the black hole from which the paper itself emanates.

Scholarly phraseology is the scientist's analog to found art. It's a welding torch that can turn bits of junk into high-priced gallery pieces. A correlative conjunction here, a prepositional phrase there, the invocation of a judicious concatenation in a third place—all these can add bread crumbs to the meat loaf of an incomplete idea, spread papier-mâché over the framework of a poorly structured experiment, or cook raw data with the speed of a microwave in the rush to publication.

The need for such a guide, long felt throughout the various professions, has finally been met. Even as Nicolai Copernicus circulated sketches of his Sun-centered planetary system to test reactions before he dared publish *De revolutionibus orbium coelestium*, so today scholars are passing back and forth private papers that elucidate the meaning of scholarly phrases. These loose leafs—dittoed, creased, and duplicated until they are a *reproductio ad absurdum*—serve as a reminder that there is no phenomenon safe from the scholar's inquiry.

The most apt of these scholarly phrases have been excerpted here. To these, the author has added his own feeble contributions (translation: "The best of the lot are mine").

A GUIDE TO WHAT THE SCHOLAR WRITES AND TO WHAT IT MEANS

"This paper will omit a review of the more recent literature in favor of . . ."
I haven't checked to see if anything's been written on this since my dissertation.

"In broadest outline, her theory can be summarized as follows . . ."
The dust jacket of her book states . . .

"Various authorities agree . . ."
I overheard in the hall at the last meeting . . .

"It is well established in the literature . . ."
I've read only the studies that support my point of view.

"No space will be wasted summarizing the well-known contributions of . . ."
He hogged the limelight in graduate school, and he ain't gonna do it here.

"It is suggested that . . ."
I've always wondered if . . .

"The implications are clear . . ."
The implications aren't *clear.*

"The results warrant additional research for a more complete
   understanding of . . ."
I think I can squeeze another paper out of this.

"It is the opinion of this writer that . . ."
*Just once I'd like to write 'this leads to the inexorable conclusion
   that . . .'*

"It was observed that . . ."
My seven-year-old noticed . . .

"Any cursory review of the literature would show that . . ."
My hunch is . . .

"This finding has not yet been fully incorporated into the general
   theory of . . ."
I hope my next graduate student will make sense of it.

"In the interest of stimulating a free flow of ideas, this paper
   will state a few major issues for consideration by . . ."
It's too late to make any sense of this mess.

"I will not insult you by telegraphing the conclusions to . . ."
I will not embarrass myself by revealing my own confusion.

"No discussion would be complete without reference to the well-
   known contributions of . . ."
I need another footnote for this page.

"There is some anecdotal evidence that . . ."
I talked to one person who said . . .

"What we now believe is that . . ."
It occurred to me in the shower this morning . . .

"It has long been known that . . ."
I can't find the reference.

"A definite trend is evident in . . ."
These data are practically meaningless.

"Of great theoretical and practical importance . . ."
It's interesting to me.

"While it has not been possible to provide definite answers to
these questions . . ."
The experiment bombed, but I still hope to get it published.

"Three of the samples were chosen for detailed study by . . ."
The results of the others didn't make any sense.

"The typical results are shown . . ."
The best results are shown.

"It is believed that . . ."
I think . . .

"It is generally believed that . . ."
I've talked two of my colleagues into agreeing that . . .

"Correct within an order of magnitude . . ."
Wrong.

"It is hoped that this study will stimulate further investigation
into . . ."
*This is a lousy paper, but so are all the others on this miserable
topic.*

"Thanks are due to Joe Blotz for assistance with data gathering
and to Jill Plutz for valuable discussion . . ."
Blotz did the work and Plutz told me what it meant.

"A careful analysis of recoverable data . . ."
Three pages of notes were obliterated when I knocked over a glass of beer.

"A statistically oriented projection of the significance of these findings . . ."
A wild guess.

"I am not aware of any research that successfully refutes this hypothesis."
I am not aware of any research that successfully refutes this hypothesis.

There is a subset of phrases, employed mainly by proposal reviewers when they evaluate proposals. They can guide us in interpreting the results of proposal reviews.

"The proposal lacks detail in many critical aspects."
I didn't read any more than the abstract.

"The principal investigator seems unaware of similar efforts elsewhere."
I'll never recommend this guy for a nickel until he cites my work.

"This proposal makes many unwarranted assumptions.
If she pulls this one off, the rest of us will look like a bunch of dumbheads.

"The hypothesis should be narrowed."
If I can't follow the proposal, how will I ever understand the results?

"Facilities are inadequate."
This one should be done in my laboratory.

A Note on the Author

ROBERT A. LUCAS is the associate vice-president for graduate studies and research at California Polytechnic State University, San Luis Obispo. Since 1981 he has written the column "Grins in the Grants Office" for *Grants Magazine*. He also contributes regularly to the National Council of University Research Administrator's *Newsletter* and conducts workshops nationally on grant proposal writing and combating writer's block.